ALISON HAMMOND'S

BLACK
IN
TIME

ALISON HAMMOND'S

BLACK IN TIME

THE MOST AWESOME BLACK BRITONS FROM YESTERDAY TO TODAY

PUFFIN

PUFFIN BOOKS
UK | USA | Canada | Ireland | Australia
India | New Zealand | South Africa

Puffin Books is part of the Penguin Random House group of companies
whose addresses can be found at global.penguinrandomhouse.com.

www.penguin.co.uk
www.puffin.co.uk
www.ladybird.co.uk

First published 2022

001

Text copyright © Alison Hammond, 2022
Illustrations by Tinuke Fagborun

The moral right of the author and illustrator has been asserted

All opinions are the author's own or those of experts. The author has taken great care to
check factual accuracy and permission to use expert content.

The links to third-party internet websites in this book are controlled and maintained by
others. These links are included solely for the convenience of readers and do not constitute
any endorsement by Penguin Books Limited ('Penguin') of the sites linked or referred to, nor
does Penguin have any control over or responsibility for the content of any such sites.

Typeset in Avenir / Text design by Perfect Bound Ltd
Printed and bound in Great Britain by Clays Ltd, Elcograf S.p.A.

The authorized representative in the EEA is Penguin Random House Ireland, Morrison
Chambers, 32 Nassau Street, Dublin D02 YH68

A CIP catalogue record for this book is available from the British Library

ISBN: 978–0–241–53231–7

All correspondence to:
Puffin Books, Penguin Random House Children's
One Embassy Gardens, 8 Viaduct Gardens, London SW11 7BW

ALISON

For Aidan – who I know will love that such an important book is his to keep forever. Love you, son. And for my niece and nephews, Matt, Jasmine and Kamran.

EMMA

For black and brown people everywhere throughout all time. We have always been here. We belong. We are worthy. Tell your stories, use your voice and lift up others!

CONTENTS

INTRODUCTION

Hiya! Alison Hammond here! Welcome to my book!

Y̶ou might have seen me on the telly, talking to famous people and asking them EVERYTHING and ANYTHING!

I love getting to know about different people and hearing their life stories . . .

… and I don't just mean celebrities (although, who doesn't want to know what Idris Elba wears on his day off, or what will.i.am has for breakfast?!), but *everyday* people too. Sometimes it's the people you don't know much about who turn out to be the most interesting of all. And that's exactly what this book is about. Although you might not have heard of the people I'm going to tell you about, they *should* be really famous because they have all done

AMAZING things! And it's going to be my pleasure to tell you about them.

You may have heard people talking about Black Lives Matter – a movement that started in the USA some time ago, but that came to the attention of the world following the tragic death of George Floyd in 2020. Suddenly, conversations about racism were happening more openly and honestly than before, with people wanting to see real change. Personally, I found myself deeply affected, and the terrible things that were happening made me think about my own son and my own family.

Then my thoughts turned towards education and history, and who I'd learned about at school. Who *were* the positive Black role models I could look up to? I knew some names, but the people who came to mind were American: Martin Luther King Jr. and Rosa Parks. Did I know much about our own Black history right here in Britain?

But, Alison, you might be thinking, ***you went to school ages ago! Of course we learn about Black people in history lessons these days! We learn about Nelson Mandela and Malcom X.***

But the thing is, if you only learn about a few individuals then you can't really understand or appreciate how Black people fit into the story of

Britain as a whole. If we only focus on the same people, then it's difficult to recognize Black people as a part of something bigger and it makes it hard to understand how much they contributed to our British society – which is a lot!

So, let me ask you a question:

When you really think about it, which Black people could you name from our British history? Mary Seacole? Ethel Scott? George Bridgetower? Pablo Fanque or Sislin Fay Allen? Have you heard of these people?

No? That's OK, cos until a year ago, I had no idea who most of them were either! But I decided it's never too late to learn, so I set about finding out more. Not just because I'm super nosy about other peoples' lives (although I am, ha!), but for my son and all the kids now who are probably thinking the exact same thing as I did at school – that history wasn't made by people who looked like me. Now, I'm definitely no historian, or even an expert writer, so when I decided to delve into the past, I knew I'd need some help! Step up, Emma Norry, an amazing writer who also happens to be *really* good at finding out all sorts of facts. Alongside Emma, the incredible historian Olivette Otele (who you'll learn more about later!) has also checked anything we weren't sure about. Even with that help, there are still some people who the historical records just don't tell us much about. This is pretty annoying, but until someone invents a time machine so I can go back and interview them myself, studying history means just accepting that there are some things we'll never have all the details about. Instead, we have to use what facts we do know to figure out as much as we can.

So now, here I am, sharing everything I've discovered with YOU! I've been on a right old journey, I can tell ya. I now know that Black people have always been here in the UK – throughout every period of history. Our arrival on to British soil didn't start and end with the *Windrush* in 1948. And our contribution to society is . . . well, it's just amazing. For example, did you know that without the bird-stuffer John Edmonstone, Charles Darwin might not have gone on to make his famous discoveries? Or that there was a Black musician who gave Beethoven a run for his money? And a Black trumpeter who stood up to the fearsome Henry VIII and demanded fair pay?

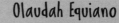
Olaudah Equiano

Ivory Bangle Lady

And I promise you this: coming on this journey with me to discover the fantastic Black people who've contributed to our society won't be as boring as some of your other lessons . . .

But that's not all! Because despite what you might think, history isn't something that stands still – it's happening all the time around us every day!

So, alongside the brilliant figures from our past, I'm also going to be speaking to INCREDIBLE people from right here and now! People who have done AMAZING things, but whose journey might have been quite different if it weren't for people paving the way ahead of them and who are now doing the same for the stars of the future – maybe even YOU!

George Bridgetower

Phillis Wheatley

Before we get started, I should also warn you that because we're delving into history there will be some attitudes that are very different to how we think today. And some of the quotes from texts of the time might use language that feels uncomfortable or wrong too. History can be tricky when we look closely, but it's important that we do, to truly reflect on the past and also to keep us all moving forward.

Anyway, enough chatter from me! Come on - let's go *Black* in time (ha - see what I did there? In the audiobook, this is where you'll hear me laughing!) with me, Alison Hammond! I'm excited! And you should be too!

THE ROMANS
27 BCE–476 CE

You probably studied the Romans at school – I certainly did. All the history books gave the impression that Romans were white guys in funny togas and helmets – gladiator-style. But archaeological evidence proves that wasn't the case. According to legend, the whole of Roman civilization started with two brothers called Romulus and Remus, who definitely did not get on. They founded Rome, which was the centre and heart of the Roman Empire.

Like loads of legends, we'll never really know the truth behind the story, but there's no denying that for around 500 years the Romans were in charge of lots and lots of countries. They conquered the Mediterranean, loads of Europe, the Middle East and North Africa – eventually the Roman Empire covered three continents! So, the Roman Empire included people from countries that we now call Egypt, Tunisia, Algeria and Morocco – which meant that Black people were Roman citizens. Yeah, let that sink in for a moment.

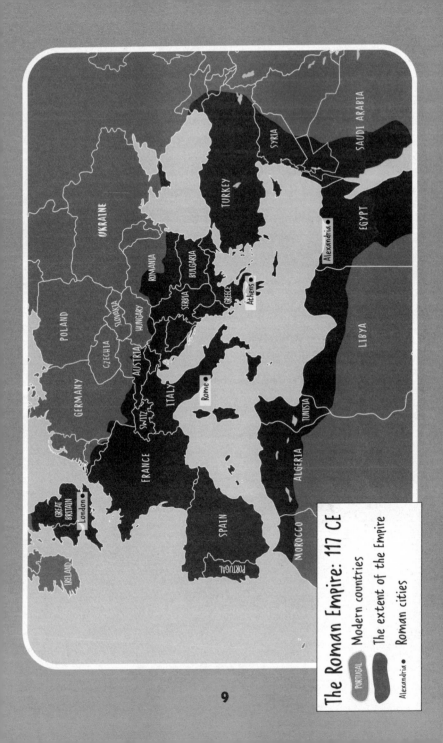

The Roman Empire: 117 CE

Modern countries

The extent of the Empire

Roman cities

PORTUGAL

Alexandria●

9

Just how did Britain fit into all this you might ask . . . Well, when it came to Britain, the Romans were pretty keen to set up home here and they invaded three separate times. The first time was in 43 CE when Emperor Claudius was the big boss.

> AKA a REALLY long time ago!

Historians mostly agree that the Romans had successfully invaded and taken control by 87 CE – so it took a while!

As the Roman Empire spanned so many countries, there was a load of travelling, with people from all over mixing and living together. North Africans would definitely have come to settle in Britain. In fact, there's evidence that the Romans didn't even really view 'race' the same way we do now. **The colour of your skin didn't mean anything about your place in society. The Romans didn't just know how to build roads – they also had some other really good ideas too!**

Now you can't really invade all those countries and get to be the boss without liking a good fight, can you? That's why the Romans had massive armies, with powerful, scary soldiers called legionaries. It was thanks to them that the Romans conquered so many places. Some of the soldiers sent to protect the area we now call England (but which the Romans called Britannia) were from North Africa. In fact, a whole troop of North African soldiers, called the Aurelian Moors, were stationed around Hadrian's Wall – which was a proper border between England and Scotland (then called Caledonia) back then – in the third century. They got their name from Emperor Marcus Aurelius. These soldiers came from Mauretania, North Africa (now parts of Algeria and Morocco).

So, there you go! The image you could have in your head of a typical Roman might not be quite right. It turns out their society was pretty multicultural, which is incredible!

To show you more about what I mean, I'm going to tell you about two important Black people from ancient times who we know a little about: **SEPTIMIUS SEVERUS** and **IVORY BANGLE LADY**.

We don't have heaps of information from around this time that we can be sure of (I suppose they don't call it *ancient* history for no reason!), but I'm going to do my best to fill you in on these two amazing people from our past.

SEPTIMIUS SEVERUS

ROMAN EMPEROR, EPIC WARRIOR AND POLITICAL MASTERMIND

WHO WAS HE? A Roman emperor from 193–211 CE.

WHEN WAS HE AROUND? The second century

WHY IS HE SO IMPORTANT? Septimius ruled over large parts of Europe, including Britain. He was the founder of the Severan dynasty, with his descendants ruling the Roman Empire between 211 CE and 235 CE.

We've all heard of Julius Caesar, haven't we? Well, some historians actually reckon Septimius Severus was the more important Roman leader.

What a name, eh? All those 'S's makes me think of a very slippery character. Was he though? Let's take a look at his life history and find out how he got to be such a VIP in the Roman Empire. Basically, he was a no-nonsense warrior.

Who was also pretty good-looking if the statues I've seen of him are accurate!

Septimius was born in 145 CE, in Lepcis Magna, one of the three major cities of North Africa (the city would now be in what we know as Libya). His dad's family were known as the **Septimii** and were **Punic** – meaning they were descended from Phoenicians who'd come from what is now known as North Africa. His mum's family were the **Fulvii**, so she was of Italian Roman ancestry. The whole Septimii family were from well-respected roots and had plenty of connections in the **senate**. So right from the start, you might have imagined big things would be in store for Septimius.

A big political institution, a bit like our parliament.

QUICK FACTS:
ROMAN SOCIETY AND RANKINGS

When we talk about the Roman Empire, we need to include Ancient Rome too, which was where it all began. The small city of Rome was founded in the eighth century BCE, almost 2,800 years ago. At first it was a monarchy – meaning the people in charge were kings and decided by birth. But then later on it became a republic, which meant getting rid of the kings and letting politicians make all the decisions. The Republic of Rome lasted for centuries and then it was all change again when it became an empire. So now all the power belonged to the emperor – the big boss; the king of kings.

Roman society had many groups; they were really keen on setting clear ranks and places for everyone. The emperor and his family sat at the top, then came the patricians (noblemen) who had all the power and were loaded. Quite a lot of people who were in this group had something to do with the military, politics or religion. Then there were the plebeians (the people) – this meant pretty much the farmers and workers. And finally, there were slaves – mostly anyone captured as a prisoner of war.

Septimius's family was almost certainly a patrician one, and that gave him certain privileges, including an education. He would have learned Greek and Latin, which were both really important to the higher ranks of Roman society, and he'd have probably studied poetry, history, geography and other stuff his family would have thought were valuable for his future life, like public speaking or politics.

They trained them up young!

Septimius stayed in Lepcis till he was eighteen, and then, like loads of us, wanted to leave home to see the world and seek his fortune! And where better to go than the heart of the empire itself? So, off he went to Rome.

The Romans were BIG on the idea of 'It's not what you know, it's who you know', and Septimius definitely had connections! A relative of his recommended him to Emperor Marcus Aurelius, who then got young Septimius in with the right people when he arrived in Rome.

Even so, success wasn't guaranteed, and Septimius really had to prove himself. In fact, his first job in Rome didn't go so well, and he returned home for a short while before going back to try again. This time he did much better at making his mark and moved up the ranks pretty quickly through hard work, but historians also think that the fallout of the awful

He was an ambitious, determined guy!

Antonine Plague – which sadly killed as many as five million, with at one point over 3,000 Romans dying every day – meant that there was less competition around for the top jobs.

Septimius might have been busy with work, but he also found time for a family life too. We think his first wife, Paccia, was also from Lepcis Magna and that they got married around 175 CE, but sadly she died in 186 CE. There isn't much mentioned about her in the history books, which is a shame. But when he became emperor, Septimius

You make statues of people you want to remember, right?

commemorated Paccia with some statues, which made me think he must have really loved her.

I reckon the statues show a softer side to Septimius that might surprise you when you read on to find out about his rise to power. But if rumours are to be believed, there's something else that shows he wasn't necessarily tough through and through because – get this – **he was a big fan of astrology**. Yep, that's right – star signs! Whenever he consulted astrologists, they always told him an amazing destiny awaited him – not a bad thing to hear, so maybe that's why he liked visiting them so much!

According to gossip, using astrology was actually how he met his second wife, Julia Domna. She was born in western Syria to an Arab family. Her astrology forecast said she'd marry a king . . . so no wonder he had his eye on her! Septimius's ambitions to rise to the top were no secret. For example, one story said that he had gone to an imperial banquet wearing the wrong clothes just so he would be given the emperor's own toga to wear. In the summer of 187 CE, when he was the governor of the Roman province of Gaul (France), Julia and Septimius got married in what's now known as Lyon.

... Signs that he was destined to become emperor one day? Maybe!

Septimius loved strong women – that's for sure! Julia was powerful and influential, although everything she did had to be behind the scenes cos of the position of women in society at the time – but she really helped him. According to records, Septimius liked her political beliefs, and Julia was involved in philosophy and writing letters. We might not know exactly what part she played in assisting him, but the fact that she went with Septimius on his military campaigns and stayed with the army in camp was very unusual at the time – no other wives did this!

There's more to come from Julia later, but you'll have to wait to hear about that because **right now, Septimius has an empire to take over!**

SO HOW DID SEPTIMIUS GET TO BE EMPEROR?

So, it's New Year's Eve 191 CE and the current emperor, Commodus, has been murdered. I know, right – not much of a celebration! At this time, Septimius was governor of Upper Pannonia (which would now be in Austria and Hungary) and commander of a large army.

Told you he worked his way up the ranks!

Anyway, the murder of the emperor got everyone planning and plotting, thinking if Commodus was out of the way, this was their chance to grab a piece of the power pie. Lots of men wanted to become the big boss and a civil war basically started; 193 CE became known as the **Year of the Five Emperors** with five men, including Septimius, claiming the title of the top job.

The first man to make a grab for power was called **Pertinax**. He was a high-ranking official in Rome at the time when Commodus was murdered, and his senior office (and probably the fact that he was actually *in* Rome) meant he was proclaimed emperor.

The problem was that very quickly Pertinax got power hungry and tried to force the people and the military to adopt unpopular rules. So, knowing

19

the Romans as we do, how do you think they dealt with him? No . . . at just three months into his rule, a small group of soldiers called the Praetorian Guard stormed the palace and murdered Pertinax too! The Guard wielded a lot of influence, behaving like the emperor's personal bodyguards and giving it the big 'I am', so while the emperor might

A quick chat over a cuppa?

have been the big boss, without their backing that power meant nothing, as Pertinax sadly learned.

While all this was going on, Septimius had travelled to Italy, and only eleven or twelve days after Pertinax was killed, he announced he'd be throwing his hat into the ring and making a bid for power. But it wasn't that easy because, remember, three other guys also wanted to be in charge! The Praetorian Guard said they'd hand over control to whoever offered them the most dosh.

Money talks, eh?

The man who offered the most money was
Didius Julianus, so he quickly took the top job. But
even though the Guard might have been happy
about Julianus paying
his way to the top,
most people thought
getting power by buying it was pretty unfair. And
with three rivals still out there stirring up trouble, it
wasn't going to be easy for Julianus.

I mean, they were the ones getting the nice pay-out!

Septimius knew that to be a proper emperor,
money wasn't going to cut it if he wanted to be
accepted in Rome. He was the closest out of the
would-be emperors to the city, so he swiftly marched
his army to Rome, gathering support along the way.

Now Septimius was in competition with **Clodius
Albinus** (who was based in Britain at the very west
of the Roman Empire) and **Pescennius Niger** (who
was based in Byzantium at the very east of the
Roman Empire). So, if it's about location, location,
location, then our Septimius was in a very good
position!

When he was about fifty miles north of Rome,
there came word that even the Praetorian Guard
had deserted Julianus, and he too was killed. His
time in charge was even shorter
than Pertinax's – just nine weeks!

Ouch!

So, two down and three to go . . .

The other good news for Septimius was that he'd already been announced as emperor by his own troops and had gained a lot of popularity, but, even so, he knew he couldn't take on both Albinus and Niger. So, in a clever move (he knew how to work this lot of power-hungry fellas), Septimius sent a message to Albinus telling him if he accepted him as emperor then Septimius would make him his second in command. Albinus accepted. Smart move by Septimius, right? Getting Albinus on side meant he would only have Niger to deal with.

With that in the bag, Septimius left Rome, went east and defeated Niger. But it didn't end there, because for whatever reason – and maybe he never really planned to go through with it at all – Septimius decided that, actually, he *didn't* want Albinus to be his deputy and told him the deal was off.

This did not go down well with Albinus (I mean, obviously) and they both ended up having a battle, with Septimius and his troops coming out the victors.

Phew! You still with me? Great!

So now, Septimius finally became the emperor at the end of 193 CE!

If I had the chance to sit down and have a cup of tea with Septimius right now, I'd ask him why he was so focused on becoming emperor that he dedicated himself so fiercely to beating the competition. Did he really think he was the best man for the job? Or maybe he wanted to make a name for himself and his family? Or was it about glory and money? Power?

It can be difficult with ancient history to understand exactly why people did what they did, especially with historians arguing over which documents are actually true or not. Even if something was written down, we've no way of knowing who wrote it or what their motives were! I mean, having learned how quick the Romans were to get into a fight or see off their enemies, I'm sure most people didn't want to risk saying anything bad about the emperor. And when you're the one in power, you can write what you want about yourself, can't you?

Like . . . I'm Alison Hammond and I'm really really great! Ha - but you already knew that, right?

HOW DID SEPTIMIUS COME TO BRITANNIA?

By this point, if I was Septimius I'd be so exhausted I'd just want a long old holiday! But now that he'd got the big-boss job, he had to get stuck in and start making some emperor-style decisions.

He decided to break up the Praetorian Guard and replace them with new recruits. Previously, the Guard had only been soldiers from Rome itself, but Septimius made the Guard *way* more inclusive and brought in 15,000 of his own mates. Why did he do this? Well, maybe he'd seen how powerful the Guard had been when they ganged up together, so he wanted to stop that happening again. Plus, by replacing members with people he knew, he'd stand a better chance of them being loyal to him.

Clever man, eh?

In 207–8 CE, around nineteen years into Septimius's rule, the governor of Britannia, Senecio, sent a message that said (roughly, we don't have the exact words):

> *'We here in Britain are being attacked from the north and are in danger of being overrun,'*

and Septimius got right on it. He was like, 'Let's build some walls'.

Did you know that the square mile of Roman London – or Londinium, as it was known back then – has walls around it that were defined by Septimius? If you've been to London, you might have even seen some remains of the walls which are still standing today – clearly, they built things to *really* last back then!

But we know by now that Septimius wasn't someone who just sat around and let people get on with things. So, in 208 CE he came to Britannia and went north to conquer Scotland (then called Caledonia) with around 40,000 men. That was the biggest army anyone had ever seen in those days.

Now, that many men are a lot to keep in check, so once again Septimius used his brains to keep them onside. He gave them a bonus and increased wages. It's interesting to wonder if he did it to get their support and loyalty, or maybe it was because he was actually on the side of the workers, and felt grateful for them fighting for him and the Empire. But whatever his reasons, it was pretty sensible! We know that in 197 CE, not long after Septimius came to power, he created three new legions, giving the army a major role and allowing them to marry! So whatever his motives, it seems Septimius always wanted

What a romantic, eh?

to make life as good as he could for the soldiers who followed him.

The border with Caledonia was marked by Hadrian's Wall, and Septimius knew that to protect Britain from being attacked he had to make sure the wall was much more secure. So as soon as he reached the border with his men, Septimius set about ordering a massive building project.

That guy sure loved walls!

He carried on with his men, pushing north, hoping to bring Caledonia under Roman rule. But it was a hard war with lots of casualties on both sides and not much progress.

HOW DID IT ALL END FOR SEPTIMIUS?

We know Septimius chose to spend his last years in York (known then as Eboracum) because he brought over his wife and sons and court.

Septimius died in February 211 CE. His funeral was a big affair. Septimius was supposed to have said to his sons on his deathbed:

> *'Be harmonious, enrich the soldiers, scorn all others.'*

But it seems that they didn't listen to his wise words because when his sons went back to Rome, although they were supposed to rule together, their rivalry carried on. And this wasn't your usual brotherly squabble. At the end of 211 CE, less than a year into their co-rule, one of Septimius's sons was killed by the Praetorian Guard – supposedly on his brother's orders. Such a shame that they couldn't just get along like Septimius wanted.

Yup, them again!

Septimius was a true warrior; he was powerful and people respected him. His legacy was to stabilize the Roman Empire following years of power struggles. He was the founder of a dynasty of emperors from his descendants. From everything I've learned about him, I can tell that he wasn't someone to mess with, what with all his power-grabbing (with help from the military), charging senators with dishonesty and plotting. But he also seemed to have a softer side when it came to his wives and to looking after the soldiers who stood by him and helped him retain power.

I wish I'd known about Septimius Severus and heard his story when I was younger – I reckon I'd have been way more into history!

TOP FIVE
FACTS ABOUT
SEPTIMIUS SEVERUS

1. He was born in 1245 CE, in Lepcis Magna, North Africa, which today would be known as Libya.

2. He loved to put his face on coins and minted a few in 208 CE showing soldiers crossing a bridge over a river.

3. He erected the Arch of Septimius Severus in Rome, which you can still see today.

4. He suffered from gout. Gout is severe pain in your joints – feet, hands, wrists, elbows, or knees. There was no cure at the time.

5. His ashes were placed in a beautiful purple urn and taken back to the Mausoleum of Hadrian in Rome, but unfortunately no one knows where they are now.

AMAZING HERE AND NOW
NICOLA ADAMS

NICOLA ADAMS *was one of the absolute stars of Team GB at London 2012, becoming the first woman to win an Olympic boxing gold medal. She went on to win a gold at the Commonwealth Games and World Championships and another Olympic gold medal before she turned professional in 2017. Nicola has received both an MBE and OBE from the Queen and has been named on more top-ten lists of influential people than I can possibly mention here. She's a total powerhouse inspiration, both in the ring and out of it!*

Your boxing career has been epic - with so many examples of you paving the way! The first English woman to win a major tournament; the first female boxer to win a gold medal for Team GB, and also the first double Olympic champion female boxer for Team GB. What do you consider to be the highlight of your career so far?

I know this gets said a lot, but I can't pick just one – that's why they do highlight reels! Of course, there was something so special about each milestone, because not every achievement is the same. But I think for most people it's the first one that always resonates the most, no matter how long it's been, which is why the Olympic gold was so special. After winning that first gold medal, I was overcome by such an indescribable feeling – I think it was a mixture of knowing all my hard work had paid off, and also that my win meant something bigger for women's boxing as a whole. At that time, female boxers were determined to bring attention to our sport, and my win was part of that. But to have been given the honour of a medal for myself and Team GB is a moment I will never forget, and it's definitely a career highlight!

You have inspired so many young girls to take up boxing, which is a sport that might not have seemed open to them before. Did knowing that you were the first female boxer to compete at such a high level for England and Great Britain add any extra pressure when you were competing? Or is it something that you tried not to think about?

What I've always loved so much about boxing, as a sport, is that once you're in the ring, it's just you and your opponent. You need to clear your mind, block the rest of the world out and focus on what's ahead. Of course, my mind would be racing in the moments leading up to a fight, and there's as much of a psychological element to boxing as there is physical. I went out there with laser focus and did the best I could in the ring. I knew what I wanted, and I went out there and got it – which, looking back, was why so many girls found it inspiring. Because women aren't always encouraged to act like that.

It is humbling to be looked up to, but I try not to think of that as added pressure. I have so many role models and mentors to thank for helping to build my confidence and turn me into the person I am today, so I'm proud if I can provide that to younger people too.

I've just shared the story of Septimius Severus, who, like you, knew how to win a battle! Had you heard about this amazing Roman emperor before? Do you think there's anything we can learn from his life?

No, I had never heard of Septimius Severus before, which is terrible when you think about it! In fact, I have to be honest – at first I thought you meant the Harry Potter character Severus Snape! I really loved reading all about him, though – I had no idea that there were Black people in positions of power in the Roman Empire. I definitely didn't learn about him in school.

You're right that Septimius clearly knew how to win a fight, and I think, like me, he knew exactly what he wanted to achieve and did everything in his power to make it happen. I think that his rise to power shows that working hard and never losing sight of your goal will really help you go places. Plus, a bit of strategic thinking when you're facing a fierce opponent can mean the difference between a win and a loss!

This book aims to shine a light on amazing Black people in British history. If you could meet anyone from the past, who would it be and why?

Anyone who knows me knows that Muhammad Ali has been one of my heroes from the start. Growing up, I would sit and watch endless replays of him winning at the Olympics, winning titles and becoming world champion. I would have loved to meet him and tell him how much of an inspiration he was – he was the main reason I wanted to become an Olympian. If I had to pick someone from British history, it would be Lennox Lewis. He is a phenomenal boxer and a big inspiration for many people getting into boxing today.

I'm a massive fan of *Strictly Come Dancing* (I loved my time on the show!) and you were part of the first same-sex couple to dance on the ballroom floor. Do you still dance and how did your boxing background help with the moves?

Being part of the first same-sex couple on Strictly Come Dancing was a great experience. Not only did it mean that I got to learn a new skill, but being in a couple with Katya meant I was doing something that had never been done before and we were making history – just like in my boxing career. It felt very special indeed. I would be lying if I said there weren't any transferable skills from boxing to dancing – quick feet from my boxing days definitely helped. You have to move fast in the ring and even faster on the dance floor. It's not called the 'quick step' for nothing! I love to dance, but I'll admit that it's less ballroom these days and more my own moves and music.

What would your top tip be for me and everyone reading this book if we wanted to become Olympic champions?

Find something you love and stick with it – really commit to it. There will be hurdles and challenges that come your way, no matter what you do, but the main difference is how much you want it and how much you're willing to push yourself to get there. You can achieve anything as long as you put your mind to it. To me, it's always been about how much I wanted it, and the desire and hunger to fight for it – no matter how many obstacles stood in my way. When you see how much a gold medal at the Olympics means to athletes, it's because that's been their life for years. It's the determination, focus and dedication that will get you there. If you put your mind to it, I'm sure you could do it, Alison!

IVORY BANGLE LADY

NOBLE WOMAN OF MYSTERY WITH GOOD TASTE IN BLING!

WHO WAS SHE? An unknown woman whose remains were discovered in York.

WHEN WAS SHE AROUND? The fourth century

WHY IS SHE IMPORTANT? Archaeologists believe her remains prove that Roman society was more ethnically diverse than previously thought. It's the job of archaeologists to find out about the past, and they do this by examining historical objects and remains.

It's amazing, really, what archaeologists can find out about how people lived in the past – even stuff like what they wore, what they ate, and what gods they worshipped – by digging up the items societies have left behind. It also means that they can give us all the goss on how things *really* were for regular people – much better than just using official records. I mean, in school, they were always going on about kings and queens, but I reckon it's more interesting to find out about us 'ordinary' people too, don't you? And the next person I'm going to share with you is an example of just how important archaeology can be for our understanding of history.

QUICK FACTS:
ARCHAEOLOGICAL DIGS

Archaeologists identify sites where they can find objects from and information about historical periods. Some ancient cities are buried deep underground.

Once they've identified a site where they think ancient remains are buried, they explore it. This is called an excavation, or a dig. Using tools like spoons, knives, brushes, and picks, they carefully try to uncover buildings, tools, weapons, art . . . anything that people used and made. The items that they find are called artefacts.

Then the archaeologists study the artefacts to understand when it was made, what it was made from and what the object was used for.

THE DISCOVERY OF IVORY BANGLE LADY

It's really tricky to guess at just how many people came to Britain during Roman times. The movements of Roman armies are well-documented, but there aren't too many records of how many regular civilians came to Britain, or even why they did. It's a real shame. Not having these records means that we don't even know the name of one of the other Black people that we know about from ancient history. That's why historians call her Ivory Bangle Lady.

Her bones were found in 1901 in York (which, you might remember from reading about Septimius, used to be known as Eboracum). They found her skeleton in a stone coffin (the proper name is a sarcophagus), and she got the nickname Ivory Bangle Lady because that's exactly what she was buried with: bangles and ivory.

At the time her coffin was uncovered, they didn't have the same high-tech forensic science we have now to discover details about her life, but they did know that what she was buried with was from the fourth century. The quality of the jewellery meant that for a century, she was thought to be an important Christian woman of Roman York, but not much thought was really given to where she might originally have come from.

It wasn't until 2010 – over a hundred years after Ivory Bangle Lady was first found – that archaeologists were able learn more about her. They analysed her facial features and evidence from the burial site and re-examined her skeleton – sixteen centuries after she died – and found out that she lived in a diverse society. Her bones proved that she was of North African heritage, making Ivory Bangle Lady the first woman of African descent found on British soil.

Incredible, right?

Knowledge about her is still pretty limited, but we know she lived over 1,600 years ago, so definitely when the Romans were in charge. **She was also young – between eighteen and twenty five –** although we don't know what she died of because there wasn't a clear cause of death.

Ivory Bangle Lady can't have been a slave or a peasant because she obviously enjoyed the finer things in life – like me! The jet and elephant-ivory bangles found with her were dated to the second half of the fourth century. They would have been very expensive, so she must have had quite a bit of money!

QUICK FACTS: ELEPHANTS AND IVORY

Nowadays we don't buy and sell ivory, but back in the day, ivory was highly desired. It was really soft, which made it easy to carve into items that wealthy people wanted. During the Roman Empire, ivory was exported from Africa and came from North African elephants. Did you know that elephants were also used in the Roman Colosseum fights? Horrible, right?

The ivory could have meant that she was from Africa. Along with the bangles buried in her coffin were also earrings, necklaces, beads and a mirror. Archaeologists also found a stone tablet engraved with the words, **'Hail Sister, may you live with God.'** So she might have been religious, which, back then, would have meant she was a Christian. In Roman times people were often buried with their most treasured possessions, so the bangles and other things must have meant a lot to her.

HERE COMES THE SCIENCE PART

Bioarchaeology is when experts study bones to discover more information – they can even prove a person's race or sex from their remains.

I find it fascinating how history and our growing understanding of ways to uncover the past can reveal hidden truths.

Like, it blows my mind to realize that examining Ivory Bangle Lady more carefully shows that Black people could have held a high-class position in Roman Britain, despite what most of us would assume from history lessons and books.

The science is dead clever and works out where someone comes from by looking at their remains in a few different ways. There's DNA analysis (not done on our Ivory Bangle Lady, sadly), looking at the shape of the skull and bones (called craniometrics), and examining chemicals left in teeth (isotope analysis), which can tell us what someone ate and drank! For example, the chemicals in Ivory Bangle Lady's teeth showed that she hadn't grown up eating the foods they ate in York, which meant she'd come from somewhere else.

Imagine if in 500 years, someone dug up my bones, examined my teeth and discovered how much I loved jerk chicken!

A bone specialist can even work out if someone is of mixed heritage because there are differences between the eye sockets, and the area between the nose and lips. The University of Reading analysed the teeth and skull of Ivory Bangle Lady, and they discovered that her skull was like skulls of other people who were found to have both Black and white ancestors. From this she was determined to have been of mixed race.

THE LEGACY OF IVORY BANGLE LADY

You can go to the Yorkshire Museum in York to see Ivory Bangle Lady's remains – as well as lots of other interesting things from Roman York. Although that might sound creepy, when I went, I just thought, wow! I was amazed to find out that she'd been wealthy in Roman times and that society then was way more diverse than I'd ever realized.

That's really her legacy. We might not know that much about her life, but she's really important because her African heritage and the fact that she was buried with such nice jewellery made historians think again about Roman society. **She helped us understand that what you did and how loyal you were to Rome was probably more important than where you came from or your skin colour – something that Septimius and his family also prove.**

Like I said at the beginning, the lives of 'normal' people can often be overlooked in favour of the 'celebrities' of their day – politicians and rulers, etc. – but if we look hard enough, ordinary people can be the ones who tell us how life was *really* lived by the majority and that can turn history on its head! This is why Ivory Bangle Lady is particularly important to our Black British history.

THE TUDORS AND STUARTS

1485–1714

OK, so the eagle-eyed among you will have noticed that we've just jumped a pretty big gap in time!

That's not necessarily because there *weren't* Black people living in Britain and doing awesome things between the Romans and the Tudors, but more that we just don't have the historical records to show what they were up to. It might sound weird, but history is always evolving (I mean, look at what we learned about Ivory Bangle Lady a hundred years after she was first found!), so who knows what we might discover about this period of time with more research!

But, for now, let's leap forward to the Tudors and Stuarts, and to two brilliant people you *need* to know about.

The Tudor period was from 1485 to 1603. After that were the Stuart times from 1603 until 1714. The one period of history that I remember learning about clearly in school was the Tudor times, and in particular Henry VIII. He was the large, boastful king who had six wives – I can still remember that rhyme about how he got rid of them all, too:

Divorced, beheaded, died, divorced, beheaded, survived!

But, again, I just assumed that royalty and the royal court had white faces. **I didn't really consider that Britain during 'olden times' could have been multicultural. We've been led to believe that our diverse society is a pretty recent development. But that's not true at all,** and we have evidence of Black people being around at the time of the Tudors and really making their mark. They are no longer going to be left out of history!

Two significant Black people during those times were **JOHN BLANKE** and **JACQUES FRANCIS**, and they're who I'm going to introduce you to next.

JOHN BLANKE

MUSICIAN BY ROYAL APPOINTMENT AND DEMANDER OF FAIR WAGES

WHO WAS HE? A talented musician in Henry VIII's court.

WHEN WAS HE AROUND? The early sixteenth century

WHY IS HE IMPORTANT? He's one of the first Black people ever recorded as existing in Britain after the Romans – and he played music for the king!

Close your eyes and imagine a Tudor party. I'm guessing you're picturing women in long dresses with headdresses, men wearing tights, plenty of food, people playing lutes and trumpets and probably not a Black person in sight?

Well, guess what? You're right about some of that, but when it comes to the royal court of Henry VII (the dad of Henry VIII, who we know so much about), it turns out that one of his musicians was a Black man! He was called John Blanke and there's actually a painting of him, so we know he existed!

> I could hardly believe it when I heard – absolutely remarkable.

John worked for – or 'served' – two kings, and I reckon he'd have seen some brilliant sights. We don't know many details about his early life, though. Just like Ivory Bangle Lady, historians need to make educated guesses about John based on the few facts and records we do have.

> Not even his real name, which is why people spell his surname in different ways - sometimes it's seen as 'Blanc' and here I'm using 'Blanke'.

It's frustrating that we don't know more about this man because, as one of the very few Black people we know was around during this time, his story must have been just as interesting as Henry VIII's, don't you reckon? Think of everything he'd have had to overcome by being a minority. But we do know some things that can tell us a little more about John and what his life might have been like.

Some historians believe that the name Blanke is a play on the words *blanc* (French) and *blanco* (Spanish), both meaning 'white'. But what we know for sure is that he had dark skin because of the two images of him that have survived. They were painted around 1511 and show us that he might have had a North- or West-African heritage, so his parents could have been Africans living in southern Europe. The UK's National Archives show us that Black musicians were popular in European royal courts (Scotland's King James IV had African drummers in his court), so John was part of a long medieval and Renaissance tradition of Black musicians.

John could have arrived in England along with Catherine of Aragon in 1501, when she was brought here from Spain to marry Prince Arthur, the oldest son and heir of Henry VII. We know her crew included trumpeters, so it's possible John was among them and if that's the case, he would have been moved into Henry VII's household when he arrived. In January 1501, there *is* a record of Henry VII paying 20 shillings to 'the new trumpet'.

Maybe this was John Blanke?

Sadly, Prince Arthur died suddenly in April 1502, which meant that his younger brother, Henry, became heir to the throne. Henry VIII's position as king was **'proclaimed by the blast of a Trumpet in the citie of London'** when his father Henry VII died in 1509. I imagine this blast of a trumpet could have come from John.

As a royal trumpeter, John would have played an important role in the king's burial, going with the procession from Richmond to Westminster Abbey, where he was buried.

Not long after his father's death, Henry VIII decided to marry Catherine of Aragon to maintain a good relationship with Spain. They were married in early June 1509, and, just a few weeks later, the coronation ceremony took place

That's right, his brother's widow!

making them officially king and queen of England.

It seems that John worked for the new king, and was given a new scarlet outfit called a livery for the coronation. It was a right old party where they celebrated for days, starting off by staying at the Tower of London.

THE WESTMINSTER TOURNAMENT ROLL

On New Year's Day 1511, King Henry VIII and Catherine of Aragon's first son was born. Henry was so excited to have an heir that he immediately ordered a massive celebration, hosting an event in Westminster that February to celebrate. There was jousting and processions and music.

And dancing too, I bet!

In the sixteenth century, people liked to record events for future generations, a bit like Instagram for the Tudor age! Henry VIII really wanted everyone to know about the fact he'd had a son, so he had the Westminster Tournament Roll made.

The roll was eighteen metres long (about the length of two and a half buses!) with paintings showing the beginning, middle and end of the whole celebration. Like taking a selfie, Henry made sure he was the main focus. On the roll, he's got his crew around him: footmen, officials, dignitaries, and six trumpeters. The trumpets are decorated with a banner bearing the king's arms. A Black man appears twice – once at the beginning and once at the end of the roll – and historians think this is probably John Blanke. He's wearing a turban; the first is green with yellow or gold, and in his second outfit, brown and yellow. Again, according to historians knowledgeable about this time period, turbans could suggest he belonged to the Islamic faith, but not necessarily. It was well recorded that Henry VIII loved dressing up and so might also have enjoyed making his court wear different outfits.

MONEY, MONEY, MONEY

Records of the payments given to musicians of the court were kept by the Treasurer of the Chamber, the person in charge of paying their wages. The earliest mention of John by name was record of a payment made by Henry VII in December 1507. Back then, John was one of eight royal trumpeters and the evidence shows that he was paid 20 shillings for the month – which works out at 8d. (old pennies) every day for work done in November. Today that would be around £430 for the month.

By Tudor standards, John was probably pretty well off. His wage was similar to what a skilled craftsman would have been paid and he'd have got food and accommodation, too. But John was definitely ambitious and thought he deserved more. Around 1510, after a senior trumpeter died, John asked King Henry VIII to give him the higher-ranking job. His petition can be seen in the National Archives. John claimed his wages weren't enough to look after the king properly, *as other your trumpets do'*, saying he wanted to serve Henry as long as he lived.

Well, you'd hope so, working for the king!

Perhaps the fact he mentions the 'other trumpeters' shows that John thought he was treated differently to the white musicians, so I'm pretty impressed that he took a stand and asked for equal pay! The king must have agreed, as John's request was successful, and his wages were doubled. I love this guy – he knew his own worth and wasn't afraid to ask the king to pay him more. And it could have ended so badly, right?

After all, we know Henry VIII had a temper and liked chopping people's heads off!

In 1512, John got married but, unfortunately, we don't have records of who John's lucky lady was. As a wedding present, Henry VIII gave him a new outfit – a gown of violet velvet and a hat. Getting a wedding present from the king shows that Henry VIII must have liked John a lot. Henry VIII's gift is the last reference we have to John anywhere, which is unfortunate for us cos I'd love to find out more. The next list of royal trumpeters in documentation is from 1514 and John's name isn't on the list.

Some historians think he died fighting in battle or found work in another royal court.

> Maybe one which paid him more!

He could have moved abroad after he got wed, or maybe he wanted to settle down. Who knows? But he remains an incredibly important person, not only in Tudor history, but in Black British history as a whole. **He shows us that not only did Black people live and work in Tudor England, but that he was someone of note too. After all, he worked at the most important place there was – the royal court!** And I love that John wasn't afraid to stand up for himself – he might have been a minority in the court, but he knew his worth.

> I was so thrilled seeing his little face in that roll!

JACQUES FRANCIS

ANOTHER TOP TUDOR AND DIVER EXTRAORDINAIRE

WHO WAS HE? An astonishing world-class deep-sea diver.

WHEN WAS HE AROUND? The early sixteenth century

WHY IS HE IMPORTANT? Jacques Francis was given an extremely important and very difficult job by King Henry VIII: to raise the sunken treasure of the warship *Mary Rose*!

Since we don't have too many facts about John, I thought I'd tell you about another fantastic Black Tudor, Jacques Francis. What we know about Jacques is also pretty limited, but his story is definitely worth telling.

Jacques was a really successful diver, and we know about him because of his involvement with the salvage of the *Mary Rose* warship.

The *Mary Rose* was part of Henry VIII's naval fleet, and, on 19 July 1545, the ship was all ready to take action against a French invasion fleet when suddenly it sank within a few minutes! **Disaster!** It swallowed around four hundred seamen and soldiers right in front of Henry VIII, who was on another nearby ship at the time.

Soon after it sank, the king ordered an attempt to get the ship back, but that failed, and no one had a clue how to raise the ship and its contents.

Then, two years later, in July 1547, a man called **Piero Paolo Corsi** was given the job of trying again. He pulled together a crack team to help him, and from historical records of the pay they received, we know that Jacques Francis was the head diver – so, the main man!

He led the diving team successfully and they recovered some important guns from the *Mary*

Rose for Henry VIII. Jacques was originally from Guinea, West Africa. It's possible that he had trained as a pearl diver in his homeland and that's why he was such a good diver.

Even though the dive was successful, drama really kicked off after it! Piero Paulo Corsi was accused of stealing from the wreckage and had to face trial. As head diver for the operation, Jacques was an important witness, and became the first known African to give evidence in an English law court! The people against his boss tried to undermine his testimony, claiming that he was a slave and that his report wasn't valid. But Jacques stood his ground and said that wasn't true, and his words were listened to by the court.

Which it wasn't!

You can see from the way that Jacques was treated by some people that although there's evidence that in Britain, at times, your skin colour wasn't as important as religion, class or talent, life wasn't necessarily easy either. And as we move forward to the next time period, we're going to come face to face with Britain's involvement in the slave trade, and a time when being Black in Britain was harder than ever.

FACT FILE: BRITAIN AND THE SLAVE TRADE

WHAT WAS THE SLAVE TRADE?

'Owning' other people is called slavery. The 'owners' make the people they've enslaved work for them, doing whatever the 'owners' ask them to do without being paid. In the past, many societies had slavery. Now, almost all societies consider slavery to be wrong. But we can't (and shouldn't) shy away from the facts. And the facts are that Britain was involved in the Transatlantic slave trade, enslaving people from West and Central Africa for three centuries. This means that when we talk about British history, we need to acknowledge this more uncomfortable side of our past.

When we're talking about slavery, a lot of attention can be focused on the British abolition of the slave trade in 1807, and then the abolition of slavery itself throughout the British Empire in 1833. But it is important to recognize that a lot of damage was done during the time when slavery was legal and accepted by so many people.

HOW AND WHY DID BRITAIN GET INVOLVED IN THE SLAVE TRADE?

Really it was all about money, power and land. In the late 1500s Britain started to realize how much money they could make by trading in cotton, sugar and tobacco and quickly set up plantations in countries under British colonial rule. British colonies were countries around the world that were under British control, with British people living there. The land, weather and climate of many of the colonies were perfect for these new goods which were in huge demand and could make you rich!

BUT HOW DID PEOPLE BECOME SLAVES?

The countries being used to grow and export these in-demand items didn't begin as slave colonies. Initially, people from England and Ireland who'd been convicted of crimes, or had debt, were sent to work in these places for a certain length of time as labourers. Guess that makes sense, right? A way to get back into society's good books by working off their bad deeds. But eventually those 'contracts' would run out, and then who was left to do the hard work? The landowners still needed people to grow, plant and harvest crops, and that's when the British started to use enslaved African workers. So, in the 1600s, it was mainly the ex-criminals doing the labour, but then over time the entire workforce became enslaved Africans who had no choice or control over the decisions and who could be enslaved through generations of families.

Massive amounts of money were being made, and as time went on, Britain started giving ridiculous reasons about why they were using slaves. Like, by the eighteenth century, instead of just being honest and admitting using enslaved Africans was the easy option, Britain was actually – appallingly – saying racist stuff like Africans were well-suited for manual work, and even that the empire was doing them a favour by giving them work to do!

WHO WERE THE ABOLITIONISTS?

The abolitionists were those who wanted slavery to end. Thankfully, not everyone was in favour of the slave trade, and eventually those voices started to have an impact. In 1807, the act to abolish the slave trade was passed. This meant that the British could no longer travel to buy more slaves. But that didn't mean that slavery suddenly ended though. It wasn't until much later, in 1833, that another law was passed to free all enslaved people across the British Empire, too.

THE GEORGIANS

1714–1837

Now we're moving forward to the period of time known as the Georgian era.

Because – get this – there were FOUR kings in a row called George – not very original, was it?!

Loads of stuff happened in Britain during this time, with BIG changes in politics, culture and people's opinions and beliefs.

Sadly, it was also during this part of history that the slave trade, which had started under the reign of Queen Elizabeth I, became an even bigger part of how Britain made its money. It's hard for us to think about people being seen as objects, treated however their 'owners' wanted and then traded for money, but that's what happened to Black people throughout this whole period.

Horrible, isn't it?

Not all of the people I'm going to tell you about next were enslaved, but you'll see that, unfortunately, because of the times they lived in, slavery nearly always forms part of their story. It's awful to know people were treated so badly, but

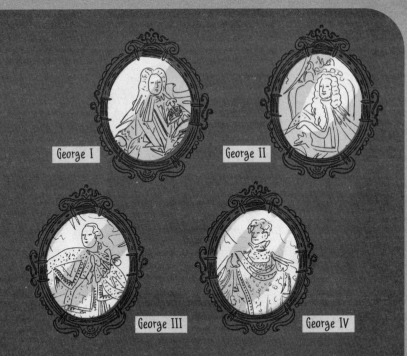

George I

George II

George III

George IV

what I love about these incredible histories is you can see these people didn't let slavery or the prejudiced opinions of society stop them from following their dreams, speaking out or trying to make a difference. I really believe that makes these people even more awesome – they didn't just roll over and give up. No! They fought and wrote and tried to change things where and when they could. And *this* is why we should all know their names. They deserve to be remembered.

So, let's meet them – come on!

IGNATIUS SANCHO

THE ORIGINAL TRIPLE THREAT: POET, MUSICIAN AND ENTREPRENEUR!

WHO WAS HE? A brilliant man who had skills when it came to poetry, music and business sense!

WHEN WAS HE AROUND? 1729–1780

WHY IS HE IMPORTANT? Ignatius was born into slavery but challenged perceptions and pushed boundaries throughout his whole life, eventually owning a successful business and becoming the first Black person to vote in Britain.

Lots of historical records can be really limited on what they tell us about people's early lives, and Ignatius Sancho's account is definitely one of these. He was born in 1729, a time when slavery was legal. Although slavery included lots of different kinds of work, like being sailors or dock workers in Britain, many people were enslaved to help with importing valuable sugar and tobacco products from America.

And, even though it's shocking to think about now, back then Black people were seen as a novelty by white people, and it was 'trendy' to have a Black maid or butler. Thankfully, however, not all Black people were slaves in the eighteenth century.

Over his life, Ignatius made a name for himself as a composer and poet, as well as speaking out against the slave trade. And so, in 1782, a couple of years after Ignatius's death, a guy called **Joseph Jekyll** wrote a biography of Ignatius.

When he wrote the biography, Joseph was unknown and at first his name wasn't even on the book! But he went on to become a well-known politician and lawyer, and so eventually he added his name as author.

We can't completely trust lots of what Joseph wrote, because who knows what his motives might have been or where he got his information – there isn't even any proof that the two men ever met!

But we do have letters that Ignatius wrote himself to try and check the book's information against. One example of something that doesn't match is that Joseph says Ignatius was born on a slave ship, but Ignatius himself claims to have been born in Africa.

So, while it's impressive that Ignatius has his own biography, having actual letters means we can learn about the man himself from his own pen!

SO, WHAT *DO* WE KNOW?

Like I said, Joseph's biography said Ignatius was born on a slave ship coming from Guinea, West Africa, to Cartagena, Colombia. But research shows that back then ships didn't take that route, so it's likely that this isn't true. Ignatius wrote in one of his letters in 1780 that he was born in Africa, but that's really all we know for definite. Other information from those early days is all over the place, too. Joseph says Ignatius was baptized by a bishop, but in those days there wouldn't be any reason for Ignatius to be baptized, especially because he was enslaved, so that is also unlikely to be true.

So, his early life is pretty patchy, but we do know that when he was around two years old, Ignatius was brought from Colombia to England by his 'owners'. He was given to three sisters from Greenwich, London. Remember before I said how Black people were a novelty at this time? Well, he was probably treated like some sort of pet by these three women, which is awful.

In a letter he wrote to a writer he really admired, Laurence Sterne, Ignatius says:

> '. . . the first part of my life was rather unlucky, as I was placed in a family who judged ignorance the best and only security for obedience . . . a little reading and writing I got by unwearied application. The latter part of my life has been through God's blessing, truly fortunate, having spent it in the service of one of the best and greatest families in the kingdom — my chief pleasure has been books, philanthropy I adore.'

The sisters weren't happy about having to teach him to read and write, but the 'greatest family' he talks about, the Montagus, were.

John Montagu had been the governor of Jamaica and was also a duke, so he was a pretty important man. One of his houses was in

Blackheath, London, which was near the house in Greenwich where Ignatius had been placed with the three sisters. John and Ignatius met by accident, according to the historical records, and John took an interest in Ignatius. He encouraged his education by giving him books. After John died in 1749, according to Joseph, the sisters threatened to send Ignatius to the Caribbean, but Ignatius asked John's widow, Mary, for help. She hired him as a butler and he worked in her house for twenty years, right up until she died in 1751.

Mary must have liked Ignatius as much as her husband had because in her will she left him seventy pounds and a further small amount for every year following. That doesn't sound like much, does it? But back then it was around the same as twenty thousand pounds! Not too bad, eh?

Unfortunately, Ignatius turned out to be not great at money management and spent a lot of the cash.

I mean, it makes sense, right? He was a young man who had just come into money, so you can't blame him for wanting to have a bit of fun!

Joseph claims that Ignatius also tried to be an actor round about now, but he had a speech impediment, which, at that time, made getting acting jobs really hard.

So, Ignatius carried on working for the Montagu family, this time as a butler for George, John Montagu's son-in-law.

In December 1758, Ignatius married Anne Osbourne, a West Indian

I bet dinner round theirs was full-on!

woman. They had loads of kids – six or seven. It's obvious just from looking at Ignatius's letters and how often he mentions Ann that he was a real family man who loved his wife and kids.

Aw!

Even though he was married, he stayed working with the Montagus until 1773. And in 1768, when the famous painter **Thomas Gainsborough** came to paint a portrait of the Duchess of Montagu, he also painted Ignatius. This portrait now hangs in the National Gallery of Canada, and you can look it up online. It's amazing – Ignatius really has some presence.

In 1773, after he'd stopped working for the Montagu family, Ignatius was left a small income by them. This time he was really sensible – I think he'd learned from his early days of not saving money. Ha! He invested in a small grocery store that he ran with his wife, Ann. I bet they made an excellent team!

Their shop where they lived and worked at 20 Charles Street, Westminster, is marked with a **HISTORICAL PLAQUE**.

QUICK FACTS: HISTORICAL PLAQUES IN BRITAIN

A plaque is a permanent sign, made from ceramic, stone or metal, which is installed in a public place. A plaque is there to remind us of the link between a particular place and a historical event or person.

The Nubian Jak Community Trust (NJCT) was set up in 2006 specifically to focus on raising funds to make sure that plaques and sculptures remember and celebrate the historic contributions of Black and minority ethnic people in Britain and beyond.

The shop became well-known for a couple of reasons. Firstly, writers, artists, actors and politicians came for a good old gossip. **The shop**

also became a tourist attraction because rich people thought having a Black shop owner was a novelty. We know that's appalling, but at least that brought in customers, and helped Ignatius and Ann stay in business. People would go there to buy essentials like tobacco, sugar and tea.

A Black man owning his own house and business was pretty incredible, and even though he was still not seen as equal to a white man, being a property owner *did* come with its own privileges. At that time, to be eligible to vote you had to be a man

If you could see me, I'd be rolling my eyes at this!

More eye rolling! Women getting the vote didn't happen until 1918, and even then it wasn't all women - there were still lots of restrictions)

and you also had to own property. So, because he owned a house, Ignatius was eligible to vote. In 1774, he did just that, becoming the first Black man to vote in British parliamentary elections.

And that wasn't Ignatius's only 'first'. He wrote music throughout his life, and he wanted to share his tunes!

How awesome is that?

He became the first Black man to publish music. Four collections of his survive today – for the harpsichord, violin, German flute, and mandolin. You can find people performing his music on YouTube!

As he got older, Ignatius became quite poorly with lots of aches and pains, asthma, and something called gout, too (which inflames your joints and in those days was super painful). Remember that Septimius also suffered from gout? Ignatius's bad health meant that sometimes he couldn't get out and about to visit his mates, so instead he wrote lots of letters to keep in touch with them. He also wrote to newspapers and public figures, often encouraging the end of slavery.

Having these letters from the man himself is great, because we can get more of an idea about how Ignatius saw himself and how he wanted the world to see him, too. It's by reading his letters that we get a real sense of who he was.

Ignatius became famous for his letters even while he was alive, thanks to the ones he wrote to the writer Laurence Sterne. The letters, like the one I quoted earlier, were included in a book of Sterne's own letters published in 1775. In them, Ignatius asked Sterne to write about the issue of slavery and to use his writing and influence to help abolish the slave trade:

'That subject, handled in your striking manner, would ease the yoke (perhaps) of many — but if only of one — Gracious God! — what a feast to a benevolent heart!'

Sterne actually spoke out against slavery in some of his work, so perhaps Ignatius did make an impact on him.

Ignatius died on 14 December 1780 and is buried in the grounds of Westminster Abbey. He was the first Black British man to have an obituary in a British newspaper. It read:

'About six yesterday morning died suddenly, Mr. Ignatius Sancho, grocer, and tea-dealer, of Charles-street, Westminster, a man whose generosity and benevolence were far beyond his humble station. He was honoured with the friendship of the late Rev. Mr. Sterne, and several of the literati of these times.'

Just like his dad, William was a trailblazer!

After he died, Ignatius's son, William, took over the shop.

He turned it into a printing and publishing business. In 1782, a noblewoman called Frances Crewe provided funds for William to publish a book of 160 of Ignatius' letters and it soon became a bestseller. I love the idea of William sharing his father's legacy and that so many people wanted to hear what Ignatius had to say.

Not bad, eh?

Ignatius Sancho was born into slavery. Yet just take a moment to think about how his life was transformed. He died a free man who owned his own business, who was well-known and respected by many for his letters, music and poetry. Due to him being so visible to the public for these reasons, he really paved the way for other Black men to vote in our elections. He showed it was possible to become a respectable business-person and homeowner. Not only that, but his son went on to use his dad's reputation to become the first Black bookseller and publisher.

I'd say that's a pretty impressive legacy.

TOP FIVE
FACTS ABOUT
IGNATIUS SANCHO

1. He was the first Black man to vote in a British general election.

2. He had his portrait painted by Thomas Gainsborough, a fashionable artist at the time, in 1768.

3. He was the first Black man to have a book of his letters published.

4. He was the first Black man to have his obituary in the British newspapers.

5. He was a loving family man with at least six children (possibly as many as eight!).

ROBERT WEDDERBURN

A REBEL WITH A CAUSE

WHO WAS HE? A political activist and abolitionist.

WHEN WAS HE AROUND? 1762–1835/36

WHY IS HE IMPORTANT? Robert was loud and outspoken about the need to abolish slavery and pay compensation or return land to freed slaves. His campaigning against slavery was such a threat to the government that he was imprisoned three times, but still he spoke out.

> *There is no one who will deny the value and importance of truth, but how is it to be ascertained, if we are not allowed the liberty of free inquiry?* — **Robert Wedderburn**

Robert Wedderburn was born in Kingston, Jamaica. His dad, James, was Scottish but had settled in Jamaica because he owned a sugar plantation. His mother, Rosanna, was an African-born enslaved woman who was 'owned' by James.

I'm using quotation marks around this term because it's terrible to apply it to people!

Apparently, James also had children with several other enslaved women who worked on his land.

This James sounds like a horrible piece of work. He sold Rosanna back to her previous 'owners' when she was pregnant, probably because she wouldn't be much good to him as a worker, and thankfully, those people had a heart and a conscience. Rosanna's new 'owners' said that her son, Robert, could be free from the moment he was born. They kept to their word and, once Robert arrived, he was baptized and even got a little education too.

Probably as a way of escaping from working on a plantation, **Robert joined the British Royal Navy aged sixteen and then, in 1778, came to London.** Travelling over on a slave ship wasn't the nicest of conditions, as I'm sure you can imagine. During the journey, Robert saw first-hand just how terrible the treatment of slaves was by the British. He'd already experienced it in the colonies, and then he witnessed it on their ships too. Unsurprisingly, this was something that deeply affected him – I mean, it must have been an awful thing to experience, especially knowing his mother had been a slave. Throughout his life, Robert campaigned to change conditions and always spoke up when he saw injustice.

He was revolutionary in the things he said and his words remain powerful to this day. In one of his essays, called *The Horrors of Slavery*, he said:

> '*I am a West-Indian, a lover of liberty, and would dishonour human nature if I did not show myself a friend to the liberty of others.*'

With no money to his name when he arrived in Britain, Robert worked as a tailor to earn a living. In London, he became interested and involved in the working classes. **He believed that all people were equal and should be treated the same,** no matter their colour or class. It was at this point that Robert joined the activist **ABOLITION MOVEMENT**.

QUICK FACTS:
THE ABOLITION MOVEMENT

The abolition movement was a group of people who didn't agree with slavery and tried to put an end to it. In 1761, the religious group the Quakers (also called the Society of Friends) decided they couldn't be involved in the slave trade. But it wasn't until a few years later, in 1787, that the Society for the Abolition of the Slave Trade (and sometimes known as other names too, like The Society for Effecting the Abolition of the Slave Trade) was actually officially set up.

An MP called William Wilberforce was very important and he was their spokesperson in parliament. He tried many times (for twenty years!) to pass the laws that would see the end of slavery, but he didn't win the vote. They had many discussions about slavery and what to do, but it was discovered that ending slavery was just too difficult to do right away.

It's easy for us to think *What? How could they say that?* Of course, keeping people enslaved was wrong, but a massive part of Britain's wealth as a country at the time relied on the items produced in the West Indies . . . and those things were harvested by enslaved people.

In 1806, another vocal abolitionist, Lord Grenville, gave a speech in which he said that the slave trade was 'contrary to the principles of justice, humanity and sound policy'. And his words struck a chord because, finally, when MPs voted on the bill to abolish the slave trade, the majority won! And in March 1807, the law finally changed. Slavery had gone on since the 1660s and it was time it ended!

So, in 1807 it became illegal to purchase slaves from Africa. But it was still a while before the trading of slaves outside of Britain stopped completely.

Robert Wedderburn found he could channel his passion into preaching, and **he became licensed as a Unitarian preacher in 1813**. He continued to be very vocal about hating slavery and used his speeches to share his views. In 1819, Robert opened a chapel in Soho, London, which became a place where people would meet to discuss how to change things for the better. But sometimes people don't like it when you speak up! And plenty of people didn't want to abolish slavery because it earned them money, so Wedderburn went to prison several times for having and sharing such strong opinions. But I like how Robert was unafraid to tell the truth about how things were. It's important to stand up for what you believe is right, even if it might not be the 'popular' view.

In 1820, Robert was charged with speaking badly against God (this is called blasphemy). He used his knowledge of the Bible to defend himself, but still got sentenced to two years in Dorchester Prison!

The time in jail gave him more time to think about how to change things, and in 1824, Robert published *The Horrors of Slavery And Other Writings*. The book was popular among other people pushing for an end to slavery, but it really wound up his half-brother, **Andrew Colvile**. Andrew was James Wedderburn's oldest son. He was also white, and James's legitimate heir.

When he had first arrived in Britain, Robert had visited Andrew and asked for some financial help, but his brother had refused! He wouldn't even accept that he and Robert were related. It sounds like he was as horrible as their dad to me! It must have been awful for Robert to be dismissed like that.

After *The Horrors of Slavery* was published, the brothers basically had a massive public row through a series of letters that were published in a newspaper called *Bell's Life in London*. Andrew once again denied Robert was a Wedderburn and threatened the newspaper editor with legal action. Even though the language is old-fashioned, have a read of this – you can still sense his outrage!

'To The Editor of *Bell's Life in London*

SIR,—Your Paper of the 29th ult. containing a Letter signed ROBERT WEDDERBURN, was put into my hands only yesterday, otherwise I should have felt it to be my duty to take earlier notice of it. In answer to this most slanderous publication, I have to state, that the person calling himself Robert Wedderburn is NOT a son of the late Mr. James Wedderburn, of Inveresk, who never had any child by, or any connection of that kind with the mother of this man . . . I have only to add, that in the event of your not inserting this letter in your Paper of Sunday next, or of your repeating or insinuating any further slander upon the character of my father, the late Mr. James Wedderburn, of Inveresk, I have instructed my Solicitor to take immediate measures for obtaining legal redress against you. I am, Sir, your humble Servant, A. COLVILLE.'

The newspaper was more on Robert's side, which was unusual for the time.

These days you can find Robert's writing online – it's free to read now because it's from so long ago. Look at the response to one of Andrew's letters he sent to the editor of *Bell's Life in London* in 1824:

'My dear brother states that my mother was of a violent temper, which was the reason of my father selling her; – yes, and I glory in her rebellious disposition, and which I have inherited from her.'

Nice bit of banter there from Robert – shutting down his brother *and* standing up for his mother at the same time!

Think of how easily all those disagreements about who belonged to whose family could have been sorted out with DNA testing these days, eh?

We don't know exactly when Robert died. Historians reckon it was before official death registers started being kept in 1837. But there are some records of a Robert Wedderborn who died aged 72 and was buried on 4 January 1835, so that might have been him.

ROBERT'S LEGACY

Robert wasn't shy about coming forward. What he did in his lifetime touched on so many different areas. He passionately believed in being able to ask questions, and in the value of human beings being treated fairly, no matter what their race, colour or class.

Robert let everyone know his thoughts and beliefs, and we should be encouraged to do the same, because that's how things will change for the better.

Tell your parents, caregivers, teachers and anyone who will listen that you'd like to know and understand more about Black people in Britain. If you tell them that you want to hear about all the wonderful things people through the ages have done in this country, then perhaps things might change. Who knows – you might get more Black teachers in schools and more Black history in the curriculum!

Maybe you could even start a school project on the people in this book who interest you. Let's keep their names alive because they're amazing. Think about how hard it would have been for them in the days when slavery was around. Even those who weren't enslaved might have been looked down on, or considered strange and foreign.

How much harder did they have to work to prove themselves?

Robert was part of the abolition movement – even though his mother was enslaved, he was born free, and so his experiences were different to others within the movement who had been enslaved themselves. Many of them wrote and published their personal accounts of slavery, talking honestly and openly about the horrible things they'd witnessed and had to go through. Thankfully, this made people begin to see them as human beings and not, as some had thought of them before, as 'cattle' or objects. One of the best-known authors is the man we're going to look at next . . .

OLAUDAH EQUIANO

AN ADVOCATE FOR CHANGE

WHO WAS HE? A former slave, seaman and merchant, and a prominent member of the Sons of Africa.

WHEN WAS HE AROUND? 1745–1797

WHY IS HE IMPORTANT? Olaudah Equiano's autobiography contained first-hand experiences of his time as an enslaved man, highlighting the truth of the slave trade. He also went on to promote the end of slavery in parliament and was fundamental in the push for change.

The early part of Olaudah Equiano's life is a little mysterious, with different accounts of his place of birth; at some point he said he was born in what's now known as south Nigeria, but according to a baptismal record he could have been born in Carolina. Royal Navy records have his birthplace as South Carolina. When Olaudah was a young man he told people he was from Carolina, but as he grew older he told people he was from Africa.

Although we don't know for sure exactly *where* he was born, there's certainly no doubt that his story is remarkable, and there are plenty of things that we *do* know that make it so.

Olaudah said that he and his sister were captured and kidnapped when he was eleven by local slave traders. The two of them were separated, and Olaudah was sold to British slave traders, taken to the West Indies then across to Barbados, then Virginia.

Poor kid, can you imagine how terrified he must have been? And how much he must have missed his sister, too?

In Virginia, he was unlucky enough to be sold again – this time to Lieutenant Michael Pascal, a Royal Navy officer. Pascal gave Olaudah a new name, Gustavus Vassa (after a Swedish king, apparently), and unsurprisingly Olaudah wasn't very happy about that! He'd been given several names before, so was probably sick of it, but as an enslaved man, Olaudah didn't really have much choice. It was common for slave owners to rename enslaved people whatever they wanted.

Can you imagine how distressing that must have been? Not only did you have to go and work for someone for no money under terrible conditions, doing everything that they told you, but you couldn't even keep your own name! What an awful world it was when slavery was legal.

Well, don't worry, we will call Olaudah by his given birth name!

Olaudah stayed on the ships for eight years. During that time he got baptized and learned to read and write. He travelled widely with Pascal, working for him during the **SEVEN YEARS' WAR**.

QUICK FACTS: THE SEVEN YEARS' WAR

From 1756–1763, the world was involved in a global conflict that spanned five continents. There was a big struggle for power between Britain and France as a part of it, and the war also massively affected the Spanish Empire, too.

Olaudah was then sold to a ship's captain in London, who took him to Montserrat, an island in the Caribbean, where he was sold *yet again*, this time to a merchant named Robert King. And thankfully, it's here that Olaudah's luck really began to change. I'm starting to get dizzy reading about all the moving around poor Olaudah had to cope with.

Robert King was a Quaker, a religion that, among other things, firmly believes all people are born equal. So, the chances are Robert felt bad about owning an enslaved man, and it sounds like he treated Olaudah pretty fairly, all things considered.

He let Olaudah do some trading on the side to make a little money for himself. And then, when Olaudah was around twenty-one and had worked for Robert for three years, Olaudah was allowed to buy his freedom. It doesn't seem right to us now that he had to pay someone else for his freedom, but for enslaved people an offer like that was usually their only chance to be free.

Anyway, Robert and Olaudah must have got on all right because Robert wanted Olaudah to carry on being his business partner. But, even though he was now a free man, Olaudah knew it was too risky to hang around the British colonies, where others might still question his status as a free man and try to kidnap him again. So, he decided to go to England.

LIFE AS A FREE MAN

London, at the time, had a growing Black community and to Olaudah it seemed he could be whoever he wanted to be here, both socially and politically. England gave him the chance to become who he wanted – for the first time ever!

I bet that blew his mind.

He paid for night classes to train as a hairdresser and took up music lessons in the French horn, but he soon realized that he could earn much more money by travelling on the sea again. One trip involved him going on an expedition to the North Pole with Charles Irving, who was an amateur scientist – imagine that, going from enslaved man to Arctic explorer!

Olaudah carried on working at sea, travelling sometimes as a deckhand, for around twenty years. During that time, he saw lots of free men being taken by force and enslaved – no one cared that technically they were free. Then one time, the same thing happened to him – he was taken! Just grabbed!

I'm sure you're thinking that surely he could tell everyone he was free and they'd have to let him go? Well, it's hard to believe now, but in those parts of the world at that time, the law wasn't on Olaudah's side. If all he had was a piece of paper saying he was free, and someone had stolen those papers, or he had lost them – then what? How could he actually prove he was a free man? Whenever anyone saw a Black person, they would have been considered enslaved or potential slaves without a second thought. That would have made life tricky for Olaudah travelling around, so it's not really surprising he was kidnapped.

Thankfully, eventually he did escape – By then he was thirty years old. Having been enslaved, becoming a free man, and then taken against his will, Olaudah began at that moment to really

> I wish I could ask him how he managed it, I bet it's quite a story.

consider what freedom was on all levels. He kept travelling, but returned to London frequently and found comfort in looking into different religions.

WHAT PART DID OLAUDAH PLAY IN THE OPPOSITION TO SLAVERY?

In 1783, Olaudah alerted an anti-slavery campaigner called **Granville Sharp** about the *Zong* massacre, which had just had its first trial. The *Zong* massacre was an appalling historical event. It's hard for me to tell you about it, but it's important that we don't look away from the truth about the slave trade.

In November 1781, more than 130 enslaved Africans had been thrown overboard by the crew of a British slave ship. The enslaved on board had become very ill, and the captain believed that arriving with a ship full of ill people meant he wouldn't be able to sell them. He was so worried about not making any money that he was willing to commit murder, and then – as if that wasn't dreadful enough – to try and claim their deaths were an accident!

When I read about this event, it really upset me. I found it difficult, almost impossible, to understand that people thought so little of human lives. How could money be so much more important?

Unfortunately, although Granville Sharp was already known for campaigning against slavery, even *he* was unsuccessful in having the crew prosecuted for murder. Despite the crew not facing justice, over time the knowledge of the massacre grew, and the anti-slavery movement argued for greater rights. In 1791, parliament stopped insurance companies from paying ship owners if enslaved people were murdered by getting thrown overboard. It wasn't justice for the lives lost, but it *was* progress, so Olaudah really made a difference by sharing the story of the awful massacre.

In 1786, Olaudah got involved with a movement that wanted to abolish slavery. He became a prominent member of the **Sons of Africa**, a group of Black men who campaigned for the end of slavery. You can imagine that after all he'd been through, he really knew what he was talking about when it came to sharing what being enslaved was like.

The Sons of Africa were a real force for change, and I'd recommend looking them up to find out about the other members. They held meetings to lecture and inform people about slavery, and wrote letters to members of parliament and newspapers. The group had such power that they were able to meet with important people in government and helped make changes to the laws around slavery.

In 1787, Olaudah was appointed as Commissary of Provisions and Stores, making him the first African man to hold a post in the British government. This was a very big deal! The project hoped to help 400 freed slaves find work and housing, and to give them a new life by relocating them.

He published his autobiography in 1789. It was called *The Interesting Narrative of the Life of Olaudah Equiano or Gustavus Vassa, the African*. Olaudah wrote about how enslaved people were branded like cattle. He talked about things that are hard for us to read about, but it was

very important because most people reading it at that time had absolutely no idea what life was like for enslaved people.

LEGEND!

Nine editions of the book were printed between 1789 and 1794, and it became a bestseller. Olaudah also went on what could have been the first ever book tour! He travelled around Britain telling his stories at abolitionist meetings for five years. He must have been exhausted, but it was all for the greater good – hearing from someone who knew exactly what it felt like must have helped the abolitionist movement.

I'm glad to say that he became a very wealthy man and had a really happy home life, too. In 1792, Olaudah married a white Englishwoman, Susanna Cullen, and they had two daughters.

Susanna died in February 1796, and a year later, Olaudah died in London, aged around fifty-two. It's a real shame that he died ten years before Britain's slave trade ended, and over thirty years before slavery was banned throughout the British Empire. After all he did to speak out about it, it would have been wonderful if he'd got to see slavery abolished.

But he left behind a fantastic legacy and his life is such an inspiring story. This was a proud Black man who refused to be kept down – he achieved success against all the odds. And hopefully he stands as reminder to all of us that we can do the same.

I know that's how discovering his story made me feel.

TOP FIVE FACTS ABOUT OLAUDAH EQUIANO

1. He was one of the founding members of the Sons of Africa.

2. A man of many talents – in his lifetime Olaudah was a sailor, trained as a hairdresser, and eventually became a writer and activist.

3. He escaped from slavery – twice!

4. He travelled the world many times and even reached the Arctic Circle as part of an expedition.

5. He played a key role in the abolitionist movement and changes to British laws around slavery.

PHILLIS WHEATLEY

THE PIONEER POET

WHO WAS SHE? The first African-American female poet to be published.

WHEN WAS SHE AROUND? 1753–1784

WHY IS SHE IMPORTANT? By following her dreams and believing in her abilities, Phillis showed that Black women were more than capable of achieving great things.

Right, it feels like we've mostly been talking about men, so I'm excited that now I get to tell you about an amazing woman!

Phillis was born around 1753 in Gambia or Senegal, but again we don't have all the details. She was born on a slave ship which made several stops within West Africa, and so we can't be sure of the precise place she was born. But, aged seven or eight, she was definitely sent to America and according to records, she was small and not very well – poor thing!

She arrived in 1761 and was sold to the Wheatley family, who lived in Boston. The Wheatleys named her after the ship she'd been on, and unlike Olaudah Equiano, we don't know what her name was before that time.

John Wheatley was a well-off merchant and tailor, and he and his wife, Susannah, had twins, Mary and Nathaniel, who were around eighteen when they bought Phillis.

It must have been obvious Phillis was clever because Mary and Nathaniel tutored her and taught her to read and write. Aged around nine years old she spoke and read English, and studied Latin and Greek, too. She read lots of poetry and was allowed to spend time learning, rather than having to do the jobs she'd been employed to.

99

Phillis wrote her first published poem when she was around fourteen!

It was printed on 21 December 1767 and was said to have been inspired by two visitors to the Wheatleys' who had told a story of how a storm had struck their ship and how they'd only just escaped disaster.

But it was the publication of *An Elegiac Poem on the Death of the Celebrated Divine George Whitefield* in 1770 that really brought her to the attention of the public.

As you can see, they didn't really have snappy titles back in those days (not like this book, eh?!).

It would have been a real novelty for the Wheatleys to have an enslaved girl who could read and write so beautifully. Some historians think that the Wheatleys supported her doing this because it made them look good. I hope it was because they were nice people, but I suppose we'll never really know. Anyway, I'm sure Phillis was happier being able to learn and write than work as hard as most enslaved people were expected to, and in cruel conditions which could have meant being starved and beaten.

Phillis really wanted to publish an entire book and not just the odd pamphlet or one-off poem, but it wasn't easy. As a young Black woman who was enslaved to a rich family, the dream of being a published author must have felt impossible!

MOVING TO ENGLAND

In 1772, a trial that became known as the **Somerset Case** took place. An enslaved man called **James Somerset** had travelled to London from America with his 'owners'. While in London, he'd tried to run away, only to be recaptured again! Lots of people thought this was unfair (including Granville

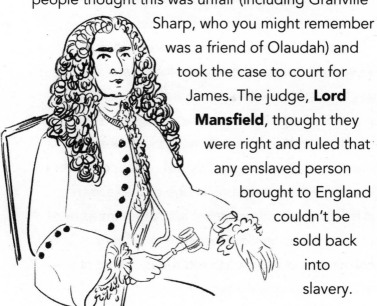

Sharp, who you might remember was a friend of Olaudah) and took the case to court for James. The judge, **Lord Mansfield**, thought they were right and ruled that any enslaved person brought to England couldn't be sold back into slavery.

You're wondering what this has got to do with Phillis, aren't you? Well, you see, the ruling didn't mean all slaves were free in England (sadly), but it *did* mean that when Phillis came to England a year later, in 1773, under English law, she couldn't be forced back into slavery!

So, in 1773, with financial help from an English countess who was keen to support her poetry, Phillis travelled to London with Nathaniel Wheatley. She was about nineteen and had come along to promote her poetry collection because, by then, she'd made a bit of a name for herself in America. She had a big list of important people to visit in London, **including the famous American Benjamin Franklin,** who was there at the time!

Her first poetry collection was called *Poems on Various Subjects, Religious and Moral*, and it was the first book ever to be written by a Black woman in America!

Go, Phillis!

It had thirty-nine poems in it and included a foreword that was signed by **John Hancock** (who you might have heard of as one of the leaders of the American Revolution) and other important men from Boston. The foreword was there to tell everyone that the men could prove the work was written by a Black woman.

That makes me so mad! Imagine being thought so little of that you had to get a bunch of men to prove your own words, thoughts and ideas were yours?

A few weeks after Phillis arrived in England, Susannah Wheatley got ill. Phillis and Nathaniel went back to Boston to look after her. Not long after that, Phillis was freed by the Wheatleys. They may have decided to offer her freedom because on the trip to England many people had criticized them for keeping her enslaved, since she'd gone about as any free person would.

Phillis' poems often explored her Christian values. The poems were very religious, celebrated America and talked about life at the time. Her poems didn't really talk about the bad stuff, and some people criticized her for this. Some also said she was influenced by the popular poets of the times and copied them too much. But that just sounds like jealously to me! For her age and situation, **she was a trailblazer by being the first female Black poet to get her work out there!**

During the American Revolution, Phillis openly supported the patriots (the ones who didn't like being ruled by Britain), and the fact she thought slavery was wrong was obvious. One of the poems she became very famous for praised George Washington, who was the commander of the Continental Army at the time, and she sent it to him in 1775. Here's a little snippet:

'Proceed, great chief, with virtue on thy side,
Thy ev'ry action let the Goddess guide.
A crown, a mansion, and a throne that shine,
With gold unfading, WASHINGTON! Be thine.'

But I'm sorry to say that Phillis didn't go on to publish any more books. We know she married a free Black man called **John Peters** in November 1778 and, though there are no historical records, it's thought they had three children together.

Phillis did try to publish a second book of poetry in 1779, but that didn't happen. She had to take a job in a boarding house to earn a living, and I imagine that it must have been difficult to work while still trying to write. I hope that she was happy, though.

Phillis died on 5 December 1784 when she would have only been in her early thirties. I know it seems like her life ended far too soon but her achievements can't be taken away from her. From her humble beginnings, she shone briefly as a poetry star. She was the first female African-American published poet and was connected to loads of well-known people who really respected her work. Her writing showed people that enslaved women were not unintelligent – that's totally obvious to us now, of course, but back then people had been led to believe that enslaved people were inferior.

So I say, go on, Phillis!

AMAZING HERE AND NOW:
MALORIE BLACKMAN

MALORIE BLACKMAN *is an incredible author who you might know from her fantastic* **Noughts & Crosses** *series, as well as countless other books, loads of which have been adapted into plays and TV series. In 2008, Malorie received an OBE for her services to children's literature, and from 2013 to 2015 she was also the Children's Laureate. How amazing is that?*

When did you have your first book published? How long were you writing before that happened?

My first book, *Not So Stupid!*, was published in October 1990. I left my job in computing just after it was released, determined to take a year out to see if I could turn writing into a full-time career. My partner and I decided we could last a year without my salary contributing to the household bills – but only a year. If it didn't work out, I'd be asking for my old job back! As I was determined that wasn't going to happen, I worked like I'd never worked before, during one of the happiest years of my life. I was stony broke, but I was doing something I loved – I was writing full-time.

Before my first book was accepted for publication, I'd written eight or nine books, all of which had been turned down by numerous publishers. It took over two years and eighty-two rejection letters before a publisher said yes. On opening the acceptance letter, I screamed in delight and danced around my hall. Oh, frabjous day! Callooh! Callay!

The *Noughts & Crosses* series is INCREDIBLE and in lots of ways turns what we think about race on its head. How did you come up with the idea and how important was it to you to write books that tackled racism for a young audience?

Noughts & Crosses was my fiftieth book. I wrote it when I felt I had published enough books in different genres and on all kinds of subjects not to be labelled the 'issues' author! When I first started my career, there was such a dearth of children's books featuring Black characters that just having black children on the book jackets felt like a statement in and of itself. I wanted my books to show ALL children that Black children were perfectly qualified and able to have all kinds of adventures too, and it wasn't just white children. But after forty-nine books, I felt the need to write something different. It was around the time of the murder of the teenager Stephen Lawrence, and it was that event that helped to shape and inform the subject matter.

In the first book, I wanted to present systemic racism in stark terms, where those with power didn't even see themselves as racist, but rather as 'upholding the status quo', because the status quo worked for them. Against that backdrop, I wanted readers to see two people – Callum and Sephy – living, loving and trying to survive. That's why it was incredibly important to me that the story was told from the point of view of both of them. It wasn't my story, it was theirs. I wanted readers to make up their own minds about the rights and wrongs of Callum's and Sephy's life choices and decisions. And I wanted readers to make up their own minds about the rights and wrongs within the society presented in the book.

I believe that adults constantly underestimate what young people are interested in and what the subjects they want to read about are. I know that as a teenager, I was trying to make sense of the world and my own place within it, so any books, TV programmes, films, music and art that helped me on that journey were not just welcomed but embraced.

I also wanted to present a realistic portrait of systemic racism as a force that blights, maims and kills. Systemic racism, particularly unchallenged systemic racism, has consequences. It was important to me not to shy away from that truth.

You were the Children's Laureate from 2013-2017, the first Black woman to be given that honour. How did you feel when you found out? What did you hope to achieve over your time in the role?

I was thrilled when the role was offered to me. I knew it would be hard work (it was!) but it was so worth it. I decided to focus my energies on encouraging teens, particularly reluctantly readers, to embrace stories and books in all their forms. As part of my tenure, we set up the YALC (Young Adult Literature Convention) as an integral part of the LFCC (London Film and Comic Convention). I wanted the YALC to be a celebration of all kinds of YA books – including graphic novels, poetry and stories of all genres. I hope in my two years as Children's Laureate that I switched on a few more young adults to the joys of reading and stories, and introduced keen readers to a wider range of authors and illustrators.

This book is all about incredible Black people which history has overlooked, including Phillis Wheatley, the first Black woman to be published in Britain. Have you heard of Phillis before? What do you think about her story?

I have heard of Phillis before and I read some of her book a long time ago, back when I was in my twenties, but I feel the time is right to revisit it. She, like so many other Black women, had to fight to have a voice, to be heard. Women like Phillis Wheatley, Mary Seacole and Olive Morris were so influential to me, particularly when I was struggling to get my first book published. It felt like whenever I stumbled or fell, they were there beside me, alongside all my ancestors, encouraging me to get up and keep going.

You've got some pretty impressive superfans, including Stormzy (OMG!). Who are you a superfan of and why?

OMG is right! When I heard Stormzy was a fan of my books, I was stunned! I was such an admirer of his long before we ever met, because he isn't afraid to be his authentic self. I admire anyone who uses their authentic voice to make life better for others. I'm a superfan of those who are not afraid of being different and who are true to themselves. And I'm a super-massive fan of Beyoncé, Will Smith and Viola Davis!

If you had to write a story featuring me, what would it be about?

First, I'd ask you, 'What one secret ability/talent do you have, or what is the one supernatural ability would you like to have? ESP, telekinesis, super empathy, telepathy?' Then I'd ask you to tell me two good things and one bad thing about yourself. And then I'd take it from there. That would be fun!

GEORGE BRIDGETOWER

THE MINIATURE MAESTRO

WHO WAS HE? A super-talented child-prodigy violinist.

WHEN WAS HE AROUND? 1778–1860

WHY IS HE IMPORTANT? George's incredible talent took him around Europe, mixing with royalty and the upper classes, as well as famous musicians like Beethoven. He was also the first Black man to be part of the Royal Philharmonic Society and broke down plenty of boundaries for Black musicians who followed him.

George Bridgetower was born in Poland in 1778. His dad was African, a former West-Indian enslaved man, and his mother was of German-Polish descent. You'll have seen a theme by now of not having all the details in the accounts of these early lives; George might have been born in February or October, but we don't know the exact date. However, his early life, when he toured as a violin superstar, has been well documented.

When George was a boy, his dad apparently worked for **Prince Esterházy of Hungary**. The prince's castle had an opera house and a private orchestra where the well-known Austrian composer Franz Joseph Haydn also worked. The Esterházys were known to be very rich with lots of influence in Austria, and they loved music and the arts.

I suppose they must have done to have their own private opera house and orchestra!

It helps to have friends in high places, right? Well, it so happens that the prince loved supporting the arts, so if these stories are true, then hanging around a famous composer like Haydn in that environment must have inspired young George.

George's first concert was in Paris in April 1789 – he was only nine or ten, so it must have been a very big deal! Can you imagine being a solo performer at such a young age? For this first appearance, his dad, John Frederick, added 'Bridgetower' to their family name. Research suggests that this was possibly taken from 'Bridgetown' which was a town in Barbados – George's father could have been from there. Perhaps he thought it sounded better than their family name, which was Polgreen . . . Anyway, whatever the reason for the name change, George was a big hit and got rave reviews – everyone loved him!

King George III even attended one of the performances and described it as 'exquisite'!

Then George moved to England with his dad. He performed in London, Brighton and Bath.

George often played at exciting venues and at court, and sometimes was advertised as **'The Son of the African Prince'**. It was his dad who was the one who liked to say this about George – he clearly understood the nature of showbiz cos this pushed up the price of the tickets to five pounds (a huge amount at the time), and to play along with the story, his dad would go to George's concerts dressed up in a turban and Turkish robes. I hope his dad was just thinking of how best to promote his son's talent and get him the biggest audiences he could, but because George was so young it's also possible that he was just taking advantage of George to make money for the family.

When George was about eleven, the Prince of Wales took a shine to him, taking him under his wing and giving him tutors. George also studied music more, getting taught by an English composer called William Attwood. He became the first violin, which means the head violinist, in Prince Esterházy's private orchestra, playing in that position for fourteen years and became a very famous and well-respected musician.

George continued to tour as well. It was during a concert tour of Europe in around 1802 that he made friends with **Ludwig van Beethoven**. I mean, how impressive is that? Beethoven could see how talented George was, describing him as *'an absolute master of his instrument'*. The two of them performed together in May 1803, and their concert included the premiere of an incomplete sonata by Beethoven for violin and piano. Since it was George who played the violin, this means that

Beethoven wrote a sonata just for George! (Although, after a row, he apparently took that honour back.)

In 1807, George got elected to the Royal Society of Musicians. What an honour – he'd really made it now, hadn't he? A few years later, he got his degree in music from Cambridge University. He did some composing there too, as well as teaching piano. He carried on performing and travelling around Europe.

George married Mary Leech Leeke in 1816. Again, we don't know too much about his final years. He died on 29 February 1860 in London.

Seeing a Black violinist wasn't something that was new in Georgian London. A French performer, Chevalier de Saint-Georges, had come before George and made a name for himself. But **what makes George so remarkable is just how young he was when he came on to the music scene. Seeing a Black twelve-year-old who was so talented perform must have been very special,** especially as at this time Black people were mainly seen as 'exotic' servants or workers, and definitely not as musical prodigies to rival Beethoven!

TOP FIVE
FACTS ABOUT
GEORGE BRIDGETOWER

1. Beethoven composed a piece of music for him.

2. George's younger brother, Frederick, was a cellist.

3. He studied music at the University of Cambridge.

4. George was elected to the Royal Society of Musicians in 1807.

5. A letter that was sent from Beethoven to George was sold at auction for over three thousand dollars in the 1970s.

AMAZING HERE AND NOW:
SHEKU KANNEH-MASON

SHEKU KANNEH-MASON *is one of the most exciting young musicians in Britain today. An incredible cellist, he's played in some of the biggest venues around the world, released two chart-topping albums and even performed at the wedding of the Duke and Duchess of Sussex in 2018 – how brilliant! And musical genius is clearly in the genes, as Sheku's six siblings are all uber-talented musicians too, and Sheku performs with them regularly while also pursuing his solo career. For someone who is only just in his twenties, I'd say that's all pretty impressive and inspiring, wouldn't you?*

Just like George Bridgetower, you were a bit of a child prodigy! When did you first start playing music? What made you pick the cello?

I started playing the cello at the age of eight. I was fortunate enough to grow up in an environment where there was always music being played and one day I went to an orchestral concert and was instantly drawn to the cello, and the rest is history . . .

You've been in some incredible competitions, including facing off the judges on *Britain's Got Talent!* Do you get nervous when you're performing?

I feel a huge responsibility to the music and the audience when I perform and this is something I take seriously and enjoy, so I suppose the answer is no, I don't actually feel nervous.

You won BBC Young Musician of the Year when you were just sixteen, and were the first Black musician to EVER do so. Do you feel like winning took on a different meaning because of that?

Not really. It was simply a case of entering a competition that I was aware of, working hard and then being really overjoyed to win it!

This book is all about sharing the stories of amazing Black people who are often overlooked in our history. Had you heard of George Bridgetower before? What do you think of his story?

Yes I had heard of him, of course, and it's a fascinating story. And there's also the intrigue of Beethoven's 'Kreutzer' violin sonata that was originally dedicated to his friend George Bridgetower but then went to the French violinist Rudolphe Kreutzer instead.

What's your proudest achievement to date and what's on the wish-list for the future?

There are no individual occasions and the answer to both these questions is general rather than specific. I've really enjoyed so many of my performances and likewise there are so many things to look forward to in the future. I like the idea of improving as a musician and sharing music with as many people as possible.

If you had to pick one piece of music to play to me, what would it be and why?

It would be the Elgar Cello Concerto. It's a wonderful work that I love playing and am lucky enough to have recorded.

JOHN EDMONSTONE

DARWIN'S TAXIDERMY TEACHER

WHO WAS HE? John was born into slavery, but gained his freedom and became a well-respected scientist and taxidermist.

WHEN WAS HE AROUND? 1793–1822

WHY IS HE IMPORTANT? John taught at the University of Edinburgh and one of his students was Charles Darwin. He ran his own successful business and was a tutor and mentor.

John Edmonstone was born in Demerara in South America in 1793. Demerara sounds familiar, doesn't it? That's because it's the place demerara sugar is named after! Although, as with lots of regions, it's no longer called that and is now instead part of somewhere called Guyana.

John was enslaved on a timber plantation which belonged to a Scottish politician called Charles Edmonstone. Charles had a friend called **Charles Waterton**, who would often come and stay at the plantation.

Back then, all the men seemed to be called either John or Charles - not too original, hmm? I bet they got confused all the time about who people were speaking about!

Charles Waterton was a biologist who had developed new ways of keeping the skins of birds. Doesn't sound too animal-rights friendly, but remember that it was all in the name of science! It seems that John helped Charles out on one of his visits to the plantation, going with him into the nearby rainforest to collect bird specimens.

Charles also taught John how to skin and stuff birds – this stopped them going rotten in the

tropical conditions. He carefully removed their skin (yuck!) and slowly hardened it with a chemical mixture as he thought this method made the specimens look more natural.

Course, I'd argue that maybe not being killed and stuffed in the first place would keep the birds looking natural, but you know, that's just me!

Anyway, in 1817, Charles Edmonstone returned home to Scotland and brought John with him so he could continue to help him with his work. Around 1822–23, they both moved to Edinburgh, where John, using the skills he'd learned, started work as a bird stuffer. Although we aren't sure if John was a free man when he arrived, on entering Scotland he automatically gained his freedom because owning slaves hadn't been allowed in Scotland since 1778 – Scottish laws were WAY ahead of the curve, with slavery outlawed there twenty-nine years before the abolition of the slave trade in England.

So, by 1823, John was a free man and living in Edinburgh. He made a decent living by working for the University of Edinburgh's zoological museum while living near the university. He was very good at his job and became known for it; once he even preserved a fifteen-foot-long boa constrictor – that definitely got him a lot of attention!

In December 1824, John met **Mary Kerr**, and in the National Records of Scotland, there is evidence of a contract of marriage between a John Edmonstone and Mary Kerr.

It was about this time that **Charles Darwin** (yup, another Charles!) came to the University of Edinburgh to study medicine. He soon realized that he didn't really enjoy studying corpses to learn about the human body because it made him feel ill. As time went on, Charles decided he was more interested in the natural world and geology. His interest in these areas grew, and he'd go to talks and do his own investigating.

Charles heard about John and his interest in birds and went to study with John every day for two months! And in Charles' autobiography, although John isn't mentioned by name, he does remember the hours of conversation they had and recalls:

'. . . a negro lived in Edinburgh, who had travelled with Waterton, and gained his livelihood by stuffing birds, which he did excellently: he gave me lessons for payment, and I often used to sit with him, for he was a very pleasant and intelligent man.'

It has to be our John that he was talking about!

Charles Darwin

Charles Darwin went on to become one of the best-known scientists, well, ever! He wrote a book called *On the Origins of Species,* which introduced the idea of evolution and natural selection, and changed people's thoughts around science completely. Who knows, perhaps Edmonstone's experiences of life in the tropical rainforests of South America inspired Darwin and some of Darwin's discoveries? It's clear from the amount of time they spent together that Charles thought he could learn a lot from John!

Unfortunately, after 1843, all traces of John Edmonstone, or any possible family he might have had, vanish, and we can't find any further trace of him!

I suppose that's history for you – sometimes it can be frustrating because we don't know what happened next.

I just really hope that John went on to live a happy life whatever he did. And who knows, maybe Darwin invited him to his book launch!

MARY PRINCE
VOICE OF THE VOICELESS

WHO WAS SHE? Born into slavery, Mary Prince went on to share her story in an autobiography that became a bestseller.

WHEN WAS SHE AROUND? 1788–c.1833

WHY IS SHE IMPORTANT? Mary's autobiography is the only account of slavery we have written by a Black woman (and she got help writing it down by another woman, rather than a man!) and she also inspired a push for change in parliament.

Mary Prince was born in Bermuda around 1788. She lived quite a happy life with her mum and siblings. Even though both her parents were enslaved, they were 'owned' by different people, which is why they didn't all live together.

Mary's mum 'belonged' to Charles Myner and then, when he died, she was sold to another family, the Williams', to work as a house-servant.

Mary also worked for the Williams', but as she grew up in the household, she was treated almost like a sort of pet to one of their daughters, Betsy (probably in a similar way to how those three sisters treated Ignatius!).

In her own words about this period of her life, she said:

'This was the happiest period of my life; for I was too young to understand rightly my condition as a slave, and too thoughtless and full of spirits to look forward to the days of toil and sorrow.'

This lasted until Mary was around twelve, and then the Williams family had money problems and sold her for only thirty-eight pounds to a man called Captain John Ingram. Her sisters were sold to different enslavers, so poor Mary had to say goodbye to her entire family!

Then, in 1815, Mary was sold again, to John Adams Wood who lived in Antigua. During the time she was 'owned' by Mr Wood, Mary met a free Black man at her church, **Daniel James**, who was a carpenter. I imagine that going to church every week must have been a sweet relief for Mary and probably the only chance she got to really relax and be herself! It was also at church that she learned to read.

In 1826, Mary and Daniel got married. Now, usually enslaved people weren't allowed to get married without permission from their 'owners', but that obviously didn't stop these two! Mr Wood was often away travelling, and it was during one of his trips that Daniel and Mary got married. The trouble

> I mean, don't get me started . . .

> I love the fact that they went ahead without Mr Woods's consent – good for them!

was, apparently Mr Wood got pretty annoyed that Mary hadn't asked his permission, and even though Mary even offered to 'buy' her freedom so she could be with Daniel, Mr Wood refused to set her free – I'd guess partly out of spite and partly because Mary was such a good worker.

Because of the law, there wasn't much Mary could do, so she had to keep working for the Wood family.

In 1828, the Woods planned a long trip to England and Mary asked to go with them. They agreed but it seems that Mary might have had a secret plan . . . After a few months in England, she asked to be freed a second time, and when the Woods refused, Mary just left! I know that sounds like a bold move that could get her into trouble, but she was living in England remember? So the 1807 Slave Trade Act meant she was allowed to legally walk free because she was in England now, even though Mr Wood 'owned' Mary when they were in Antigua.

So now Mary was free – hooray! But she faced a new problem of being alone with no way to support herself.

Sadly, life really didn't work in favour of women like Mary during these times. Even the choice of going back to Antigua to be with her husband wasn't an option. Firstly, she had no money of her own and secondly, the moment she stepped on to Antiguan soil, she'd be classed as enslaved again, and no longer free. When she'd left the Woods, they'd written her a bad reference (no surprises there!), which meant that no one else would hire her for work, so luck was definitely against her.

Perhaps for comfort or for company, Mary started to go to church in England. And she says of these days:

'A woman of the name of Hill told me of the Anti-Slavery Society, and went with me to their office, to inquire if they could do any thing to get me my freedom, and send me back to the West Indies. The gentlemen of the Society took me to a lawyer, who examined very strictly into my case; but told me that the laws of England could do nothing to make me free in Antigua. However, they did all they could for me: they gave me a little money from time to time to keep me from want; and some of them went to Mr. Wood to try to persuade him to let me return a free woman to my husband; but though they offered him, as I have heard, a large sum for my freedom, he was sulky and obstinate, and would not consent to let me go free.

This was the first winter I spent in England, and I suffered much from the severe cold, and from the rheumatic pains, which still at times torment me.'

After a few weeks she started working for **Thomas Pringle**. He was a secretary at the anti-slavery office in London where Mary had gone for help. The anti-slavery office was a place which offered help to Black people in need.

Thomas Pringle

Thankfully there are good, kind and helpful people in this world! Thomas Pringle was one of these. He offered Mary a job as a servant. After being encouraged by Thomas, Mary decided to write her autobiography and he helped her with this.

Mary wasn't in a position where she'd been taught to write; it was only through church that she had some basic knowledge of reading. So, Thomas arranged for her to tell her story to another woman who wrote it down for her and then he edited it. With Thomas's help, Mary found a way to share her own story.

In 1831, *The History of Mary Prince* was published while Mary was living in London and working for Thomas. After the book came out, some people tried to say horrible things about Mary, Thomas and the book itself. Mr Wood complained about how he'd been described and what Mary had said about him, and he even took Mary to court! But it didn't matter – Wood lost his case against her and the book became a bestseller. The publication of it added to the ongoing conversations about slavery in the West Indies.

In the book, Mary shared her feelings about being sold at aged twelve and how upsetting it was to have gone through those times. She describes vividly her memories of the auction where she was sold: her mother crying, being examined and handled, watching her sisters being sold off. She also describes the beatings.

Just imagine if this was you being taken to an auction and sold! Think how scared and sad you'd be. And it could have been us if we lived a few hundred years ago . . . It's awful, isn't it?

But Mary spoke out, and she spoke her mind. Her words are heartbreaking:

'Slavery is hard . . . too hard and I would rather go into my grave.'

Mary's powerful story was the first account of a Black woman's life as a slave ever to be published in Britain. Her story gave descriptions of the brutality and unfair, cruel treatment that slaves experienced. Even though Mary tried – through the courts and writing petitions to parliament – to get her freedom, she was unsuccessful. Her voice and story are unique in our historical records; we have many accounts from men about what life was like being enslaved, but Mary's is the only one by a Black woman. Her memoirs are important because while Mary's story is unique to her experiences, her words give us an insight into what the lives of countless other Black women who were sold into slavery might have been like. She speaks for herself, but she also speaks for hundreds of other women whose stories have gone unrecorded and unheard. It's vital that she's remembered for her courage and persistence.

We don't know what happened to Mary in her later life, but the 1833 Slavery Abolition Act would have meant that Mary would have been able to return home to Antigua if she wanted, without risk of being enslaved again.

I'd love to think that she took that trip and found her way back to Daniel to spend the rest of her life free and happy. She deserved a happy ending like that!

TOP FIVE FACTS ABOUT MARY PRINCE

1. Mary's is the only personal account published about what life was like as an enslaved woman.

2. In 2020, it was announced that Mary Prince Day would be celebrated annually in Bermuda on the last Friday of July to recognize Mary's contribution to the abolition of slavery.

3. There is a bronze Nubian Jak Community Trust plaque dedicated to Mary in Bloomsbury, London.

4. In 2018, to mark Mary's 230th birthday, she was the subject of a Google Doodle!

5. In 1829, Mary was the first woman to present an anti-slavery petition to parliament.

THE VICTORIANS

1837–1901

In 1837, the run of Georges on the throne ended and Queen Victoria stepped up to take the crown. Victoria went on to reign for over sixty-three years, which at that time was longer than any previous British monarch.

> I mean, Queen Elizabeth II SMASHED that record, but even so, sixty-three years is a long time to be in charge, isn't it?

In the Georgian period, slavery had a big impact on the people we've met and other Black people like them. However, under Queen Victoria's rule, the rapid expansion of the British Empire taking over and colonizing countries really became a key factor in how Black Britons were seen and treated. Great Britain became the largest imperial power in the world!

FACT FILE: THE BRITISH EMPIRE

You might have learned about the British Empire in your history lessons, but when I was at school, it wasn't really talked about. Basically, Great Britain used to be the boss of many different countries all over the world – even though we're just a tiny island.

British armies travelled around, invaded countries and then forced the people who were already living there to follow British rule. All the places where this happened became known as the British Empire. Yeah, not very fair, is it? It was going on for AGES before Queen Victoria came to the throne – for example, the British took over places in North America in the 1580s and Jamaica in 1655, but it was under Queen Victoria's reign that it really picked up speed, and the empire grew and grew. We weren't the only ones doing it either: countries like France, Russia and Spain all had their own 'claims' to countries around the world.

Thankfully, times have changed, and over the years, countries came out from under British rule to become independent again. Though it sometimes took ages – it wasn't until 1962 that Jamaica had independence!

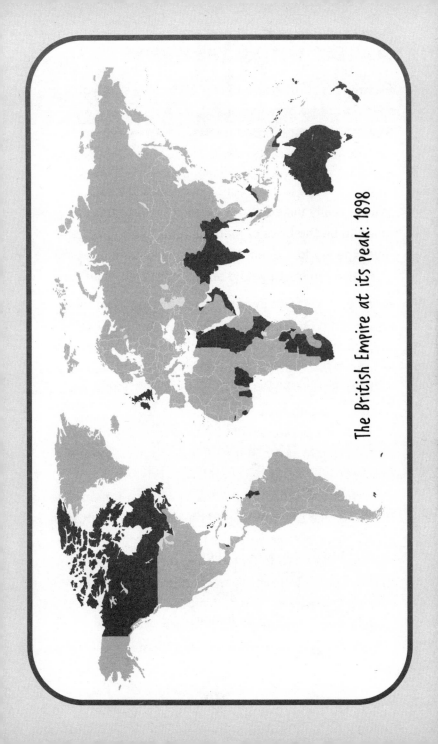

The British Empire at its peak: 1898

SLAVERY WITHIN THE EMPIRE

From everything we've talked about, I'm sure you've worked out by now that though it would be nice to think that slavery ended neatly in 1807, when the Act for the Abolition of the Slave Trade was passed in parliament, that was definitely not the case. People still illegally trafficked Africans, even though they might get fined up to a hundred pounds (which would be loads nowadays – over nine thousand pounds!) if a slave was found stowed away on a ship. There was also a 'loophole' in the act that meant some areas of the British Empire were excused from the law. It wasn't until the 1833 Slavery Abolition Act that slavery completely ended throughout the British Empire. After that, people who'd been enslaved could go back to where they were born, safely, without any danger of being recaptured and mistreated.

I know it's unpleasant to focus on slavery. It's really difficult to talk about in lots of ways, but if we don't talk about the amazing people who existed back then, who rose above the odds to achieve remarkable things, spoke out and helped pave the way for others going forward, then we're just living in denial of our past. We need to face it head on. So yes, some of these stories are *really* awful, but it's important that we know them, and also highlight the stories of people who at the time had no voice at all.

Slave traders were very focused on making money

from selling Africans into slavery. Money talks, right? And there was a lot of money to be made. But, during the late eighteenth century, people were getting more and more concerned about how enslaved people were treated. They couldn't pretend it wasn't happening anymore. And when slaves were freed, some of those previously enslaved people described what their lives had been like as slaves by writing their stories.

I'm only giving you the headlines here, of the slaves whose stories we have recorded. But when you're older (or even now!) maybe you'd like to research more deeply about them or read their accounts of their lives written in their own words. We're just skimming the surface in this book.

We've read about some fantastic men who campaigned against slavery and enabled real change, but where were the women, you might wonder? We know that times were difficult for women in Victorian times – this is before the suffragettes got us the right to vote – but what was life for a Black woman? Doubly difficult, right? Mary Prince's autobiography is the only account we have from a Black British enslaved woman. Although we might not want to know the details and may prefer to move on from thinking about people being treated as property, her story is very important, and her name should definitely be on your lips.

So let's meet some other incredible Victorians, too.

MARY SEACOLE

EMPATHETIC ENTREPRENEUR

WHO WAS SHE? A British-Jamaican nurse who saved many lives during the Crimean War through the founding of her British Hotel, which treated injured soldiers behind enemy lines.

WHEN WAS SHE AROUND? 1805–1881

WHY IS SHE IMPORTANT? Although her legacy and impact were largely forgotten for nearly a century following her death, Mary was voted the greatest Black Briton in 2004 and has a statue dedicated to her in Paddington, London.

Now, let's talk about another awesome Black Briton – another Mary! This time it's Mary Seacole, an incredible nurse. My mum was a nurse and she told me all about Mary Seacole when my classmates and I were learning about Florence Nightingale.

I've always thought Mary Seacole was absolutely amazing and couldn't understand why we didn't learn about her at school too!

Mary was born Mary Jane Grant in Kingston, Jamaica, on 23 November 1805. She was multi-cultural, as her dad was a white army officer from Scotland, and her mum was Jamaican. She had a sister called Louisa and a half brother called Edward.

Her mum used to run a respected boarding house in Kingston called **Blundell Hall** and was well-known locally as 'the doctress'; using traditional African and Jamaican herbal medicine, she healed injured soldiers who were based in Kingston. Mary learned her nursing skills and all about traditional medicine from watching her mum and by practising on her dolls. She probably learned about war and the big wide world from her dad, who, being in the army, would be used to travel.

Mary was always determined to help and fight for causes she believed in. She was given an education by an older woman who treated Mary as if she was one of her own grandchildren, spoiling her rotten. But her mum clearly also wanted her to have a business brain, so, as she was growing up, Mary was also shown how to look after the hotel.

Clever Mum!

Mary wrote about her own life and adventures in her autobiography, *Wonderful Adventures of Mrs Seacole in Many Lands*. She actually wrote the book much later in her life when she needed to make some money, but I'm mentioning it here as it's so helpful for us to be able to learn more about Mary's life from the lady herself. I'm going to make the most of having that intel and share her words as I'm telling you about her life, starting with this bit about her mum:

'It was very natural that I should inherit her tastes; and so, I had from early youth a yearning for medical knowledge and practice which never deserted me . . . And I was very young when I began to make use of the little knowledge I had acquired from watching my mother.'

Mary wasn't enslaved, although at the time she was born, many people living in the Caribbean were. As we learned earlier, Black people were brought from Africa to work on the sugar plantations in Jamaica (and the laws didn't change until 1833). But even though Mary and her mum weren't enslaved, in reality that didn't mean much because her family didn't have total freedom or many civil rights. They couldn't vote or do certain jobs, and people's attitudes during these times could still really stink (as we'll come to see!)

Mary travelled to England a few times before she became known for her nursing in the Crimea. During those times, it was very unusual for a woman to be travelling, especially alone, which she bravely went on to do. The journey from Jamaica to London took around six weeks! Can you imagine having to be on a boat that long?

'I shall never forget my first impressions of London. Of course, I am not going to bore the reader with them; but they are as vivid now as though the year 18— (I had very nearly let my age slip then) had not been long ago numbered with the past. Strangely enough, some of the most vivid of my recollections are the efforts of

the London street-boys to poke fun at my and my companion's complexion. I am only a little brown — a few shades duskier than the brunettes whom you all admire so much . . .'

That's what Mary had to say about her trips to England – it sounds like seeing a young Black woman caused some comments, but I bet Mary wouldn't have been afraid to call people out on it!

In 1821, she went to London for about a year with some relatives, and then again in 1823 for two years. While she was in England, she ran a small business selling jams and pickles, making a small but steady profit.

It wasn't just England that Mary visited. By the time she was nineteen, Mary was one well-travelled and adventurous young woman. She'd been to Cuba, Haiti and the Bahamas; she'd buy exotic spices, jams and pickles on these trips and then use her business knowledge to sell these things back in Jamaica.

Basically, Mary Seacole was the
first Black female entrepreneur!

And it wasn't just things to sell that Mary got
from her travelling. She was also always learning
from the different places she went. She had a
curious – some might say nosy – mind, just like
someone else we know, eh? On her travels, she
found out even more about traditional medicine,
taking notes about how local plants and medicines
were used to help the sick . . . things that would
come in really useful later on in her life, as we'll see!

In 1826, aged twenty-one, Mary returned to
Jamaica to help look after the old lady who'd
helped her financially and provided for her
education when she was little. Here's what Mary
says herself about her trips and then heading
home:

149

'Before I had been long in Jamaica I started upon other trips, many of them undertaken with a view to gain. Thus I spent some time in New Providence, bringing home with me a large collection of handsome shells and rare shell-work, which created quite a sensation in Kingston, and had a rapid sale; I visited also Hayti and Cuba. But I hasten onward in my narrative. Returned to Kingston, I nursed my old indulgent patroness in her last long illness. After she died, in my arms, I went to my mother's house, where I stayed, making myself useful in a variety of ways, and learning a great deal of Creole medicinal art . . .'

Being there when the elderly lady died must have been really upsetting for Mary. I wonder if that's why she decided to stop travelling and stay at home with her mum. Maybe she just wanted to be around the people she loved and in a place that was familiar.

A few years later, when she was thirty-one, Mary met and fell in love with one of her mum's boarding houses guests, a white man called Edwin Horatio Hamilton Seacole.

What a fab name, eh?

Mixed-race marriages weren't too common then, so yet again Mary was breaking the mould. Mary and Edwin got married in November in 1836, and soon after they opened a store together selling the items Mary had bought on her travels. Unfortunately, the store they'd set up together in Jamaica didn't work out, and then Edwin, always quite 'delicate' (as Mary described him), became more unwell. Mary looked after him, but as he wasn't getting much better, they decided to go back to Blundell Hall.

Poor Mary then had loads of rubbish things happen. Blundell Hall got partially destroyed in a massive fire which spread across Kingston, and then, just a year later in 1844, Edwin died. Although Mary got a lot of offers to remarry, she stayed single (and why not? I love how independent she was!). Mary's mother died soon after that, too.

The way Mary coped with her grief was by getting on with things and working even harder. Along with her sister, Louisa, she supervised the rebuilding of Blundell Hall and they renamed it *New* Blundell Hall.

Now that the home business was back up and running, it seems that Mary got another travelling bug and, leaving the boarding house in the hands of her cousin, she set off globetrotting again, busier than ever.

'I resigned my house into the hands of a cousin, and made arrangements to journey to Chagres. Having come to this conclusion, I allowed no grass to grow beneath my feet, but set to work busily, for I was not going to him empty-handed. My house was full for weeks, of tailors, making up rough coats, trousers, etc., and sempstresses cutting out and making shirts. In addition to these, my kitchen was filled with busy people, manufacturing preserves, guava jelly, and other delicacies, while a considerable sum was invested in the purchase of preserved meats, vegetables, and eggs.'

But when a **CHOLERA** pandemic broke out in Jamaica in 1850, Mary returned home to help. It was a really big deal. **The outbreak in Jamaica led to about 40,000 deaths altogether.** That was very high – a whole tenth of the island's population of 400,000 was wiped out.

QUICK FACTS: HORRIBLE DISEASES YOU'D RATHER AVOID!

Cholera, typhoid, smallpox, malaria and yellow fever all had multiple outbreaks across the world in Victorian times, and in those days, cures and medicines to help were limited, so it was pretty awful.

* **CHOLERA** is a bacterial infection caused by contaminated food or water. It made people vomit and have diarrhoea and could kill you in just a few hours.

* **TYPHOID** is also a bacterial infection spread through contaminated food and water. Typhoid was caused by poor sanitation and lack of hygiene. Adults don't just ask you to wash your hands for the sake of it, you know! It developed slower than cholera but could also kill you.

* **SMALLPOX** was another serious infectious disease and was contagious – this means it easily spread between people. It gave you a fever and a rash.

* **MALARIA** is a tropical disease spread by mosquitoes. It can be fatal without the right medicines and one mosquito bite is all it takes to get infected.

* **YELLOW FEVER** is also transmitted by infected mosquitoes. Some people suffering from it actually look a bit yellow. Symptoms include fever, headache, muscle pain and vomiting.

A doctor was staying at the boarding house, and together they helped treat many sick people using Mary's herbs and medical knowledge. As Mary tells us herself:

> 'In the year 1850, the cholera swept over the island of Jamaica with terrible force . . . While the cholera raged, I had but too many opportunities of watching its nature, and from a Dr. B— , who was then lodging in my house, received many hints as to its treatment which I afterwards found invaluable.'

Around 1851–53, Mary travelled to Panama in Central America, and helped her half-brother run his hotel there for more than two years. We know that she was a clever businesswoman, not just a healer, and she used that business sense to earn enough money from rich people paying for her treatments so that she could help the poor for free.

Isn't that great?

Eventually, Mary earned enough to open a shop that sold food too and she called it the **British Hotel**. It wasn't a hotel like we'd think of today, where people stayed overnight, but more a place to grab something to eat. She then hit on a great idea to hire a barber for the British Hotel, and it became very popular, making Mary a very successful entrepreneur.

Unfortunately, an outbreak of cholera hit Panama in 1851, just after Mary arrived. They'd already had an outbreak in 1849, so it shows just how easily the disease could return. But it didn't stop Mary. She kept running the hotel to keep the money coming in. Alongside that, using her knowledge from the outbreak in Jamaica, Mary looked after people who were sick. She even caught cholera herself. **Mary believed that having the disease helped her understand how to treat her patients better because she'd been through the same thing.**

It's obvious that Mary wasn't someone who liked to stay in one place for long, so eventually Mary left Panama and joined a gold-mining operation in New Granada.

'Altogether, I was not sorry when an opportunity offered itself to do something at one of the stations of the New Granada Gold-Mining Company, Escribanos, about seventy miles from Navy Bay . . . It is a great neighbourhood for gold-mines; and about that time companies and private individuals were trying hard to turn them to good account.'

She was hired as a cook for **Thomas Day**, who was the superintendent at the mining company and a cousin of her husband. And it was here that she first learned about the **CRIMEAN WAR**.

QUICK FACTS:
THE CRIMEAN WAR

The war started in 1853 between Russia and the Ottoman Empire (run by what is now Turkey, and reaching to the coast of the Black Sea, now part of Ukraine). The United Kingdom and France agreed to support the Ottoman Empire, which is how they ended up with troops going to fight. The Crimean War was one of the first wars to use modern explosives in battle and also to be documented by news reports and photos, so that people around the world knew what was happening. The war ended in 1856, but sadly over the three years of conflict, 900,000 soldiers died, a huge number of which were deaths from disease rather than in battle.

In 1854, Mary returned to London. Even though she was used to travelling, it really wasn't a typical thing for a woman to do back in those days, and even less so for a Black woman. Everything

I'd love to have met her - I bet she was fierce.

I've read about her proves she was not the shy and retiring type, and it sounds like no one was going to stop her from doing what she wanted.

We might wonder why she moved around so much, but Mary describes herself as 'restless', so I guess she just always wanted to be on the move to the next thing!

'My father was a soldier, of an old Scotch family; and to him I often trace my affection for a camp-life, and my sympathy with what I have heard my friends call 'the pomp, pride, and circumstance of glorious war.' Many people have also traced to my Scotch blood that energy and activity which are not always found in the Creole race, and which have carried me to so many varied scenes; and perhaps they are right . . .

As I grew into womanhood, I began to indulge that longing to travel which will never leave me while I have health and vigour.'

While Mary was in England in 1854, the War Secretary, Sidney Herbert, had asked a nurse, **Florence Nightingale**, to get a team together and to head out to help in the Crimea.

Florence Nightingale led thirty-eight volunteer nurses out to the battlefields to care for the British soldiers.

Florence Nightingale

Mary was around forty-nine by now and, having built up years of experience, wanted to help. She must have known that her first-hand experience of treating cholera in Jamaica would have been invaluable given the awful conditions on the front lines! She visited the War Office and offered to help, bringing letters from Jamaican soldiers who said how great she was at healing. You'd think they'd have leaped at her offer, right? But no.

The officials in charge were so racist and pompous that they told her she couldn't go.

In her autobiography, Mary wrote:

'But my ridiculous endeavours to gain an interview with the Secretary-at-War of course failed, and glad at last to oblige a distracted messenger, I transferred my attentions to the Quartermaster-General's department. Here I saw another gentleman, who listened to me with a great deal of polite enjoyment, and – his amusement ended – hinted, had I not better apply to the Medical Department; and accordingly I attached myself to their quarters with the same unwearying ardour. But, of course, I grew tired at last, and then I changed my plans.

Now, I am not for a single instant going to blame the authorities who would not listen to the offer of a motherly yellow woman to go to the Crimea and nurse her 'sons' there, suffering from cholera, diarrhœa, and a host of lesser ills. In my country, where people know our use, it would have been different; but here it was natural enough – although I had references, and other voices spoke for me – that they should laugh, good-naturedly enough, at my offer . . .'

But remember, Mary was no pushover! She wasn't going to take no for an answer. She might have missed a chance to be in the first group of nurses going out to the war with Florence Nightingale, but was determined to be part of the second. The problem was, Florence Nightingale was known to be very strict about training, and even though Mary knew loads, she hadn't been officially trained as a nurse.

Even then, Mary didn't give up without a fight. She knew how the army worked from her father and understood that she needed to get in front of the right people to convince them of her skills. So she kept trying, only to hear 'no' again and again! Eventually, Mary had clearly had enough and did what all strong women do – she found her own way. Nothing was going to stop her from doing what she wanted – she believed it was important and that she could make a difference.

Good on her! Sometimes you have to go your own way.

Making the most of her connections, Mary contacted Thomas Day, the man she had worked for in New Granada, and together they came up with a plan. Thomas was planning on going out to Balaklava on business, so they decided to go into business together, using Thomas' funding and Mary's smarts. They called themselves Seacole and Day, and came up with an idea to run a general store near the British camp,

I mean, not that creative, but as it's Mary, I'll let it pass!

selling all the supplies the army would need.

Here's Mary herself filling us in on how the idea came about:

'I applied to the managers of the Crimean Fund to know whether they would give me a passage to the camp – once there I would trust to something turning up. But this failed also . . . The disappointment seemed a cruel one. I was so conscious of the unselfishness of the motives which induced me to leave England – so certain of the service I could render among the sick soldiery, and yet I found it so difficult to convince others of these facts. Doubts and suspicions arose in my heart for the first and last time, thank Heaven. Was it possible that American prejudices against colour had some root here? Did these ladies shrink from accepting my aid because my blood flowed beneath a somewhat duskier skin than theirs?

> *Let what might happen, to the Crimea I would go. If in no other way, then would I upon my own responsibility and at my own cost . . . ? If the authorities had allowed me, I would willingly have given them my services as a nurse; but as they declined them, should I not open an hotel for invalids in the Crimea in my own way?'*

It makes me sad to think that she was so desperate to help and had so much knowledge that could be useful to save lives, but she was told 'no' just because of the colour of her skin. I think her words show how upset that made Mary, too; imagine knowing you could make a real difference, but that people were so prejudiced they would still turn you away. It's brilliant that she basically said, 'stuff you!' and found a way to get out there and help anyway!

Around 1855, Mary finally set off from England across the Mediterranean to pick up food, staff and medical supplies.

In her book Mary describes stopping and visiting the military hospital at Scutari on her way to Crimea. She had happy reunions with soldiers she had known before in Jamaica. She had been given a letter of introduction by a doctor she knew in England, so that she could stay the night at the hospital on her way to the front and meet with Florence Nightingale:

> 'A slight figure, in the nurses' dress; with a pale, gentle, and withal firm face, resting lightly in the palm of one white hand, while the other supports the elbow – a position which gives to her countenance a keen inquiring expression, which is rather marked ... She has read Dr. F—'s letter, which lies on the table by her side, and asks, in her gentle but eminently practical and business-like way, 'What do you want, Mrs. Seacole – anything that we can do for you? If it lies in my power, I shall be very happy.'

It's amazing to think of those two incredible women meeting for the first time – I'd have loved to have been in that room! I also like the way that Mary describes the meeting, and the fact that Florence wanted to help Mary, too. They were both there for the same reason, after all.

Mary and Thomas set up their general store just outside where the fighting was and decided to call it the British Hotel. Soldiers

> They called it the same name Mary had used for her store in Panama – a nice reuse of branding!

could buy hot food, drinks and equipment. 'Hotel' is maybe too posh a word for it – it was more like a little tin hut, made from scrap iron and wood.

The location was closer to the actual action than Florence Nightingale's official hospital by about a two-hour walk! Which put Mary exactly where she had always wanted to be: at the heart of the battles so she could help wounded soldiers. Mary often went on to the battlefield to look after the wounded, too, taking them food and using her nursing skills.

Back then, the deadliest things about war were the cold and diseases rather than the enemies

or gunfire, so Mary could really help with all the experience she'd had. The soldiers became used to seeing her around. The bright colours she wore cheered them up, and soon they started calling her Mother Seacole.

In 1856, the war ended and Mary came back to England. Unfortunately, she and Thomas had been left with expensive items they couldn't sell, and so they had to file for bankruptcy – Mary was officially broke! She'd borrowed money for the British Hotel and couldn't get another loan. And she couldn't get work, because, despite everything she had

done for the war effort and all she had achieved over her life, people still couldn't see beyond the colour of her skin.

One of the first war correspondents who wrote for the newspapers, **William Howard Russell**, made Mary more well-known. He'd covered the Crimean War in *The Times* for almost two years when he had first interviewed her. This is what he'd written about her:

> 'In the hour of their illness, these men have found a kind and successful physician, a Mrs Seacole. She is from Kingston (Jamaica) and she doctors and cures all manner of men with extraordinary success. She is always in attendance near the battlefield to aid the wounded, and has earned many a poor fellow's blessing.'

When William learned of Mary's bankruptcy, he wanted to tell the British people about all the good she'd done, so he wrote about her again in the newspaper. He reminded people of how she'd helped in the Crimea, and soldiers wrote into the paper to share their stories of how she'd helped them. Two of William Howard Russell's friends, Lord Rokeby and Lord Paget, were Crimean commanders and decided to organize a big fundraising party to celebrate Mary in 1857. It was held over four nights and over 80,000 people came, hoping to help raise money for Mary. Even Queen Victoria wrote to congratulate Mary!

Sounds fabulous, doesn't it?

But they really messed up by spending so much on organizing the party that there was barely anything left for poor old Mary!

So, doing what she did best, Mary took matters into her own hands. In 1857, yet again pushing the boundaries of what was expected of her, Mary decided to publish her life story to make some money. As I mentioned at the start, it was called *Wonderful Adventures of Mrs Seacole in Many Lands*, and William Howard Russell wrote in it: '*I trust that England will not forget one who nursed her sick, who sought out her wounded to aid and succour them, and who performed the last offices for some of her illustrious dead.*' The book was a big hit, which I'm sure was a relief for Mary as it meant she had some dosh coming in!

Mary Seacole died aged 75 on 14 May 1881. As we've seen, back in the day it was very hard for women. And Mary was *even more remarkable* because she had prejudices from others about her skin colour to overcome, too. Why Mary isn't as famous as Florence Nightingale is a mystery and a shame, although more and more children now are learning about this extraordinary woman.

There's so much more to Mary's life than I can put here, so as with all of the people I've told you about, make sure you go and look her up.

Let's give Mary the last word:

'Indeed, my experience of the world . . . leads me to the conclusion that it is by no means the hard bad world which some selfish people would have us believe it.'

TOP FIVE FACTS ABOUT MARY SEACOLE

1. Her husband was the godson of Admiral Nelson! (Yup, the guy with the statue in Trafalgar Square!)

2. She was once forced off a ship in Panama by white women who refused to share it with her.

3. When she examined a man's body after he'd died just after having dinner with her brother, she identified exactly what was wrong with him – this stopped the villagers thinking her brother had killed him!

4. Mary Seacole was awarded the Jamaican Order of Merit in 1991.

5. In 2016, her statue was put up outside St Thomas' hospital in London. This followed a twelve-year campaign to help recognize her contribution and it was the first public statue of a Black woman in the UK.

IRA ALDRIDGE

SHAKESPEARIAN SHOWMAN AND INSPIRATIONAL SPEAKER

WHO WAS HE? An actor, well-known for his Shakespearian roles, who travelled the world performing to sell-out crowds.

WHEN WAS HE AROUND? 1807–1867

WHY IS HE IMPORTANT? Ira Aldridge is the only actor of African-American descent to have a bronze plaque at the Shakespeare Memorial Theatre in Stratford-upon-Avon. He overcame racial prejudice to become one of the top-paid actors of his generation.

On 24 July 1807, Ira Frederick Aldridge was born in New York to Daniel and Luranah. **At the time Ira was born, people born in the south of the USA were still slaves, but those in the north were free.**

Ira's dad, Daniel, was a reverend at a church and Ira's family encouraged him to become a part of the church, too. But, aged around thirteen, Ira started at the **AFRICAN FREE SCHOOL**. It was also around this time that Ira started to spend a lot of time at neighbourhood theatres; no doubt this got him interested in acting and he started acting himself.

QUICK FACTS:
THE AFRICAN FREE SCHOOL

The African Free School was set up in 1787 by members of the New York Manumission Society, whose members included John Jay and Alexander Hamilton (yes, *that* one!), to give a proper education to the children of slaves and free African-Americans. This Free School was thought of as part of the abolitionist movement, because their teachings taught Black children to fight for equal rights – the idea that everyone has the same potential no matter the colour of their skin. Many more free schools went on to open.

Ira used to watch performances in two theatres. One was the Park Theatre, where he'd watch the British actor brothers Henry and James Wallack. But here, because it was segregated (meaning Black people and white people had to sit in separate sections), Ira didn't get great seats. **He preferred the African Grove Theatre, which was home to the African Theatre Company. They were the first Black African-American theatre group, and it would have been quite something for young Ira to watch Black actors in lots of different roles, everything from comedy to Shakespeare.**

By fifteen, he was hanging out regularly with the theatre company and eventually became a working actor with them.

Some curious white people would come to watch the plays, but many Americans were really racist, so there would often be trouble and protests where the African Theatre Company were performing. Some white people didn't think Black people should act, and sometimes the police had to be called because of fighting from the violent protestors! The theatre group had to stay on the move for their safety, and, eventually, the theatre company had to close because it was too dangerous for the actors and crew.

How sad is that?

Due to the racial tensions in America, Ira must have found it really hard to find ways to pursue his acting dream. It's not surprising to me that he eventually decided enough was enough and packed up to try his luck elsewhere. Around 1824, when he was just sixteen, he travelled to Liverpool with another actor friend, and, a year later, **in October 1825, he got his first professional role in the UK playing Othello** at a little theatre in the East End of London. He also performed around this time as Oroonoko in *The Revolt of Surinam, or A Slave's Revenge.*

After that, Ira continued to act in England. He toured Coventry in 1828, still trying to make a name for himself. But Ira must have made quite an impression in other ways too, because he was made manager of the Coventry Theatre for a little while, making him the first Black African-American theatre manager in Britain.

Ira was a man after my own heart; he knew how to use his platform to speak up about issues that he was passionate about. After shows he would often take advantage of a captive audience to make anti-slavery speeches, which might have changed people's minds about slavery.

All the time Ira was performing, people were protesting against slavery on the streets of London. **The Slavery Act of 1807** (which we've already heard so much about) meant that by the time Ira was born, slavery was against the law in Britain. Black people coming to England had more opportunities (and I'm sure that would've been part of the reason Ira got on that ship to Liverpool in the first place), but, even so, we know that slavery *did* continue in the British colonies until the law changed in 1833. And people's attitudes were still atrocious. So, although slavery was illegal in Britain, it didn't mean that people weren't racist or that those who had been campaigning for change and protesting were ready to stop speaking out. And Ira was one of those people who had a platform to try and make a difference.

Racist opinions meant that some people *really* didn't like the fact that Ira was on stage, just doing his thing. But, on the flip side, for others he was a really great example of what was possible.

So good on him for trying to change opinions and also for showing the next generation to follow your dream!

By 1831, Ira had become well-known, travelling to Ireland, Bath and Edinburgh, where his acting performances went down well. Ira was especially popular in some of the smaller towns he visited because they didn't get much entertainment, apart from the circus. He acted in serious Shakespearian plays, but he also used to perform a famous comedy play called *The Padlock* where he'd act silly and drunk, playing a singing and dancing servant called Mungo. So, he was able to entertain audiences with a range of different roles, showing just how versatile he was as an actor.

Ira was only seventeen when he came to London. It always astounds me how independent young people were back in those days. He was very smart too, handling his own reputation and publicity. He'd worked out that if he stretched the truth about who he was, and where he was from, he'd draw more interest. Because he was African-American, *The Times* newspaper called him the 'African Roscius', after a famous actor from ancient Rome. A little like Ignatius Sancho, who enjoyed good business due to people coming to his shop because a Black owner was a 'novelty', Ira decided to leap on *The Times* review, using it for his own benefit.

Smart man!

He made African references in his biography details that appeared on the theatre programme.

HITTING THE BIG TIME!

It was in April in 1833 that Ira got the big break that changed his life! The Theatre Royal in Covent Garden was a well-known theatre, and Edmund Kean, a famous actor playing Othello at the time, collapsed on stage. Ira took his chance and stepped in to replace him. At first, his reviews were mixed, and some people were very mean about his appearance. According to *The Times* newspaper, Ira was

'baker-kneed and narrow-chested with lips so shaped that it is utterly impossible for him to pronounce English'.

The critic mentioned his 'copper' complexion, thinking it wasn't dark enough for him to play Othello! And *The Drama* described him as

'tall and tolerably well-proportioned with a weak voice that gabbles apace.'

I guess you can't please everyone, can you?

After a while, his talent won out and his performances impressed reviewers. The *Standard* said Aldridge was

'watched with an intense stillness, almost approaching to awe,'

and that he received

'unanimous applause, waving of hats, handkerchiefs &c., &c.'

Another critic wrote,

'In Othello [Aldridge] delivers the most difficult passages with a degree of correctness that surprises the beholder.'

Ira as Othello

By the mid-1830s, Ira's star was fading a bit. He'd brought back an old play that didn't do well, and, just like when he'd left America, he decided that maybe it was time to try his luck in a new place, so he set sail for Europe to see what fortunes he could find there.

It was a good move. **In 1852, he and his family toured round Europe, and these were his glory years. Ira married twice.** He married his first wife when he was eighteen. She was a white Yorkshire woman ten years older than him, and they were together for nearly forty years until she died in 1864. Ira's second wife was a Swedish singer who he married a year later. He had four children, including two daughters who went on to become opera singers.

He was adored in Russia, and got awards and honours all over the place! In Germany, he was

given the Prussian Gold Medal for Art and Science by the king. He made **loads** of money. Wherever he performed, the theatres would be sold out. He got more positive attention in the parts of Europe where there weren't many Black people. Maybe he was a novelty – who knows? But whatever the reason, the Europeans lapped him up and Ira made the most of it by bringing in all the money he could.

Cha-ching!

The critics of German and Russian theatres really knew their Shakespeare and used to write about Ira's performances. This was a good test because they knew who was good and who wasn't! He'd 'white up' (this wouldn't be acceptable these days) to act as Richard III, Shylock or King Lear. In Russia, he earned more money than other Russian actors!

Eventually he decided to return to London; given his reputation was now so impressive, people there couldn't ignore him anymore. In 1858, he took to the stage at the famous Theatre Royal Lyceum as Othello once more, and received much more praise than he'd ever had before from English audiences and critics. Now they could appreciate his talents!

Ira Aldridge died while on tour in Lodz, Poland, in August 1867, aged sixty. Sadly, it was a sudden death, and he'd been planning a big return to the USA. It's a shame he never made it back home to show everyone there how successful he'd become, but he was really loved in Poland, and the whole town of Lodz mourned him.

Ira Aldridge's success paved the way for other Black actors, and earned him the privilege of being the only African-American with a bronze plaque at the Royal Shakespeare Theatre in Stratford-upon-Avon.

So, he was a pretty talented guy who could have taught some of our actors now a thing or two! I hope his legacy inspired many others to try and make it as an actor, and that his story inspires YOU too!

TOP FIVE FACTS ABOUT IRA ALDRIDGE

1. His stage name was F.W. Keene (he named himself Keene after the famous actor Edmund Kean, thinking it was good publicity to have the same name as someone famous – clever man!). He also named himself the African Roscius, after a famous Roman actor.

2. Some people think that it was Ira who posed for John Simpson's oil painting *The Captive Slave* (1827), which now is on display at the Art Institute of Chicago.

3. He was the first Black actor to play Othello in Britain.

4. Adrian Lester played the character of Ira Aldridge in a play called *Red Velvet,* written by Lolita Chakrabarti, Adrian's wife.

5. On 3 August 2017, a blue plaque was unveiled in Coventry commemorating Ira's work and the city's links with the African-American actor.

AMAZING HERE AND NOW:
ADRIAN LESTER

ADRIAN LESTER *is a British actor who has starred in blockbuster movies (including a Bond movie – OMG!), hit TV shows and also performed in theatres around the world. He's won numerous awards for his work and has been awarded an OBE by the Queen in recognition of his outstanding achievements!*

How old were you when you first started acting? Did you always want to be an actor?

I started singing at first, in St Chad's Cathedral choir in Birmingham. That was my first sense of any kind of real, regular public performance. It's a bit of a cliché but like so many others, I found my voice in church.

When I was at school, the idea of learning about Black history didn't occur to people. And yet, in this book there are so many amazing Black people who

I'd have loved to have known about. How important do you think learning about Black history in school would have been for you?

It would have made an immeasurable difference to me. I would have had a different and much truer sense of my own self-worth. I didn't associate Black people with history because the discoveries and achievements of that culture wasn't in the history books I was given, or used as any source material for what I was taught at school. But now I know that people from the African diaspora have had their place in world history overlooked and ignored. Learning about people who looked like me and my family would have completely changed my young perspective of history and how it related to me.

Ira Aldridge is someone you have learned a lot about over your career, and you've even portrayed him in a play! What do you think about his story and about the fact that he's still largely unknown?

How could I go through my schooling, secondary education, then go to RADA and work for ten years in the business and have never heard the name of Ira Aldridge? He was a pioneer for Black actors, having huge success at a time when people who looked like him were seen in some circles as less than human. At a time when slavery was accepted and legal. This country would not be the country that it is without the contributions of people like you and me and our bloodline. If we're talking about William Shakespeare and the amazing actors who have brought his plays to life over the centuries, then we have to hear the name Ira Aldridge.

I mentioned that you've played Ira in the theatre before, which is amazing! If you could play anyone else from history, who would it be and why?

The answer to this question changes from day to day. But, at the moment, I would look to the French writer Alexandre Dumas and his father General Thomas-Alexandre Dumas. I've been thinking about the battles, the sword fighting and the brain that gave birth to *The Three Musketeers* and *The Count of Monte Cristo* – swashbuckling adventures shot through with historic fact.

Your career has been phenomenal! You've starred in both big TV shows and blockbuster films as well as winning lots of awards for your work on stage. What's the one piece of advice you'd give someone starting out?

It's very hard to give generic advice, really, because everyone has very specific talents, but also worries and concerns when they are starting out. I would say that whoever you are and whatever it is you think you have to offer, always look after what you consider to be a weakness in your abilities. This means that every day, you have to be honest with yourself. You have to use your own eye to pick apart your abilities and make a commitment to use every opportunity you can to get better. In all honesty every job I take only serves me if it gives me the opportunity to be a better actor after I've completed it.

PABLO FANQUE

*EXPERT HORSEMAN AND CIRCUS OWNER
WHO ENTERTAINED THE QUEEN*

WHO WAS HE? A famous Victorian equestrian, acrobat and circus owner.

WHEN WAS HE AROUND? 1810–1871

WHY IS HE IMPORTANT? Pablo Fanque was the first Black circus owner in Britain, drawing huge crowds for his own act but also becoming a successful businessman, too.

The circus in Victorian times was a popular and cheap method of entertainment. Of course, now we understand that this sort of entertainment, especially one which often used animals to perform tricks, is very cruel and outdated, but throughout history popular opinions change as people become more educated.

I've just told you all about Ira Aldridge, who toured the country performing in plays, but some smaller towns didn't even *have* theatres, so visiting a travelling circus might have been the only kind of entertainment for children and families. **Pablo Fanque** was an incredibly successful circus owner and performer who was on the scene at pretty much the same time as Ira. They might have been very different types of entertainers, but they both made HUGE strides in this area for Black people in the early 1800s.

There was no Saturday-night telly in those days, poor things!

Historians think that Pablo's dad might have been a butler, and that Pablo could have been one of more than six children, but some details are sketchy. We definitely know that when he was only eleven, Pablo became an apprentice to **William Batty**, who owned a travelling circus and was one of the most successful and famous circus owners around – but we might never know how Pablo got the apprenticeship in the first place.

Pablo must have showed huge talent immediately because Batty himself led his training, taking Pablo under his wing. **Pablo made his first appearance at William Batty's circus in Norwich on Boxing Day in 1821** as the 'Young Darby', and he went on to become a brilliant horseman as well as learning rope dancing and acrobatics.

Pablo stayed with Batty for a few years before joining another circus – this one run by **Andrew Ducrow**, who had a very famous show at the time. This could have been where Pablo perfected his horse tricks and riding because Ducrow was famous for working with horses. After a while, Pablo moved on again, bouncing around and going wherever he fancied, trying out work in different places. Eventually he went back to William Batty's circus.

In 1834, Pablo performed in Liverpool at the Royal Amphitheatre, and newspapers described him as 'loftiest jumper in England'. It was around then that he really started to get a name for himself as a tightrope walker and horseman. He did this trick of jumping on to horseback over a coach 'placed lengthways with a pair of horses in the shafts, and through a military drum at the same time'.

I'd loved to have seen that, wouldn't you?

At the height of his fame in 1847, Pablo even performed on the London stage. His debut was an amazing hit and the *London Illustrated News* said:

> 'Mr. Pablo Fanque is an artiste of colour, and his steed . . . we have not only never seen surpassed, but never equalled . . . Mr. Pablo Fanque was the hit of the evening.'

The horse was called Beda, a black horse who Pablo had bought from Batty.

Long before he hit the London stage, Pablo had dreams of owning his own circus and becoming his own boss. It took him years of working in other people's circuses to get enough money together, and, by the time he finally made it happen, it was

1841 and he'd been working for over thirty years! I think that's a brilliant example of not ever giving up on your dreams, isn't it?

So, Pablo started his own circus with a clown mate of his, W.F. Wallett. They only had two horses to start with, but Pablo worked hard and, over the next six years, he managed to get many more horses. It was during that time he met his wife, Susannah, and started a family, so he was a busy man!

From what I've read, he was a larger-than-life character – probably a bit like me, so I reckon we'd have got along and had a right old giggle!

He had a reputation for being a showman who knew how to entertain. He also treated his employees with respect and kindness. There are records showing how he helped the poor by raising money for them. That's actually what's really great about so many of the people whose stories I've shared with you – when they could, they tried to give back to anyone in need. I guess when you've had to work hard to be recognized for your achievements, you want to make sure that you help other people on their way.

Over the years, Pablo's circus grew and became more successful. He even had the brainwave to get in the really well-known acts around that time, like a famous boxer called **Jem Mace**, who Pablo knew loads of people would want to come and see.

The circus travelled all around England, Scotland and Ireland, but was best known for touring the Midlands and northern England. Just like when it came to the acts he hired, Pablo was also pretty ahead of his time when it came to publicity. Lots of other circuses at the time relied on word-of-mouth alone, but Pablo decided to do things like handing out flyers and creating posters advertising his shows, letting people know where and when to find them.

Promo like that sounds really obvious now, but lots of other people at the time didn't do half as much as Pablo - he definitely knew how to pull in a crowd!

But while he was becoming a big success, Pablo's life also had its share of sadness. The biggest tragedy of all was when his wife, Susannah, died in a terrible accident during a circus performance featuring their son in March 1848.

In those days, sometimes temporary theatre buildings, known as amphitheatres, were set up to host big events. At this particular performance, their son was on the tightrope, and the gallery completely collapsed. Six hundred people were sitting in the gallery at the time, including Susannah. Heavy wooden planks landed on Susannah, and Pablo rushed her to a nearby hotel where a doctor was staying, but tragically there was nothing he could do.

There was an investigation into what had happened. It turned out that builders had started taking down the theatre by removing supporting beams, but then they'd stopped and not mentioned it to anyone. So when Pablo had taken over the temporary theatre for a few weeks, he'd been told – and *sold* – the theatre as being good to go, even though beams were missing. But health and safety regulations weren't exactly a thing in those days, and no charges were ever pressed.

Poor Pablo! I bet he felt truly terrible.

Running a circus wasn't an easy job, either. Can you imagine putting up and taking down heavy canvas tents in all weathers? And always competing with other circus shows which might be bigger and better?

At one point, Pablo had to try and get money back off a performer who'd gone bankrupt, as Pablo had lent him a bunch of horses and stuff. He didn't always get his money back, and sometimes he was forced to sell off things.

A few years later, Pablo married again. Elizabeth Corker was a woman from Sheffield who rode horses in the circus. She was much younger than Pablo and was only twenty-two when they married. They had two sons, George and Edward (who became known as **TED**). Like his other children, both boys joined the family circus, and Ted also went on to become a well-known boxer.

I'll tell you more about Ted in a mo!

Just like Ira, Pablo must have struggled being a Black man making his way in a world dominated by white people, but from everything we know, he also seems to have been accepted by

Elizabeth and Ted

the circus and loved by the general public.

After Pablo died, the Reverend Thomas Horne, chaplain of the Showman's Guild, wrote: *'In the great brotherhood of the equestrian world there is no colour line, for, although Pablo Fanque was of African extraction, he speedily made his way to the top of his profession. The camaraderie of the Ring has but one test: ability.'*

Unfortunately, Pablo died with no money at the age of seventy-six in Stockport. But thousands of people lined the streets to show their support of him. The hearse had a band, followed by Pablo's favourite horse, four coaches, and his family and friends.

TOP FIVE
FACTS ABOUT
PABLO FANQUE

1. Pablo's real name was William Darby, which is why he was called The Young Darby during his first performances.

2. The clown W.F. Wallett, who was a business partner and good friend of Pablo, once performed for Queen Victoria, as did Pablo!

3. Pablo often gave money to support those in need, including putting on benefit performances to raise money for his performers and their families.

4. One of Pablo's posters inspired John Lennon to write 'Being For the Benefit of Mr. Kite!' for The Beatles in 1967.

5. Pablo has a blue plaque in Norwich commemorating where he was born.

LIKE FATHER, LIKE SON: TED FANQUE

When the First World War broke out, Ted Fanque was a well-known performer in the circus. Ted wanted to fight but the War Office had said he was 'too old' – even though doctors had said older men were fit enough to fight. But Ted decided to stand up for what he thought was right and not let anyone or anything get in his way! I wonder if watching his dad succeed helped him to do this? He wrote a letter to *The World's Fair* newspaper in 1915 to argue his case, which was pretty salty! Here's what he said:

THE PROPOSED BATTALION OF MEN OVER FORTY-FIVE

Sir, – You will, no doubt, remember last November you kindly inserted in your paper a notice re a battalion of men 45 and over. Well, sir, I am sorry to say that we have been rejected...

The high military authorities are reluctant to employ anyone over 35, but fully appreciate our patriotism and we receive through E. S. Day, Esq., a badge and a certificate stating that: '―― was enrolled in this battalion which volunteered for any kind of service at home or abroad.

The battalion being refused by the War Office, though a thousand doctors said the men were fit to go through a campaign. – Signed, etc.'

Well, Mr. Editor, we can at least walk about feeling proud to think we are not one of the shirkers although over 45, neither need we blush with shame when we hear anyone recite the following lines: –

So Kitchener plans in his London town,
  French is Standing at bay,
Jellicoe's ships ride up and down,
  Holding the sea's highway.
And you that loaf where the skies are blue,
  And play by a petticoat hem;
These are the men that are fighting for you,
  What are you doing for them?
Bravo, then, to the men who fight,
  To hell with the men who play;
It's fight to the end for honour and friends,
  It's a fight for our lives to-day.

Poor us, and still the posters announce 'Your King and Country Need You.' Wouldn't it be better to announce 'A Grand Sale of Red Tape, for full particulars apply at the War Office.' – Yours, etc.,

EDWARD CHARLES PABLO FANQUE.

AMAZING HERE AND NOW
ANDI PETERS

ANDI PETERS *is one of my favourite TV presenters and has had success both in front of and behind the camera. Right now, you might know him for being a regular on morning TV, but he first hit TV screens in the late 1980s presenting children's TV. Aside from his top presenting skills, Andi has also been the force behind some HUGE shows like Channel 4's T4 (the show that pretty much paved the way for the channel E4 to exist!) and Top of the Pops. He's an absolute legend and an all-round entertainment superstar, so I'm excited to grill him about his career!*

One of your first jobs in TV was presenting Children's BBC, which always looked like so much fun! You were the first Black person to present that slot, and since then you have gone on to become the first Black presenter for lots of other shows too. Did you realize when you were starting out that you were trailblazing?

No, I've never really thought of myself as trailblazing. I stated presenting in the 1980s – first on CITV in 1988 and then on to CBBC in 1989. I knew I was the first Black person to get those sorts of jobs, but I've never really thought of myself as trailblazing. When you use that word, I think of the people who first hired me – taking what would have been seen as a 'risk' by putting me in front of the camera on huge mainstream shows. During my time in the Broom Cupboard on CBBC, I was on TV every day, broadcasting to up to 12 million people – and to think that that many people switched on their television and saw a Black person is incredible!

One of the funny things I remember is to do with make-up. Whenever I got my make-up done for a show, I noticed there were lots of different shades of foundation available for the white presenters, and that they were always running out of stock. In contrast, there was only one shade for Black skin, but because there were so few Black presenters – probably just me, Lenny Henry and Moira Stewart – it never ran out! I think it was small things like that that made me very aware of the fact that there were just not many people who looked like me appearing on TV.

Even today, there are still very few Black people who lead entertainment shows in this country. I think I could probably name around five or six people – including you, of course, Alison! So, there's still a long way to go before we have real representation on television.

As well as being in front of the camera, you've also done LOADS of producing and creating shows too, working on things like the brill T4, Top of the Pops and Shipwrecked. Do you prefer being behind the scenes or front and centre?

I think I prefer being on television. I get a real sense of fulfilment talking to people in the street who come up and say hello and that they like what I do. When I tell people about the work I've done behind the scenes and the shows I've worked on, there's a recognition, but there's not the same sense of immediate joy that you get from being in front of the camera.

I'm so proud of the shows I have created or have been involved in bringing to TV and genuinely love producing, but actually being on TV is where I prefer to be.

Like you, Pablo Fanque knew how to entertain a crowd, and he also used that knowledge to create and put on his own shows by setting up his circus. Had you heard of him before? What do you think of his story?

I actually haven't heard of Pablo Fanque – which is why it's so great that written this book and showcased all these incredible Black people from our past! I thought his story was fascinating, and you can really tell that he was willing to go the extra mile to be a success and make a name for himself – no matter the hurdles in his way or the tragedy that life threw at him.

Pablo sounds like a brilliant entertainer, which is something I can really respect – he knew what people were looking for and drew in the crowds. Sometimes people think that entertaining or being funny is easy, but actually it's hard work and something you have to work at to get right. I also like that he was clearly very business-savvy and didn't want to work for someone else, but instead he saw his own worth and became his own boss. It's all about doing what you do well and standing by your talent. I can definitely get on board with that motto!

Again, like you, Pablo made a name for himself in an entertainment industry dominated by white people, so he had to fight even harder to be a success. During your career in TV, have you seen things change when it comes to representation? And what changes do you hope to see in the future?

Representation has changed over the years. I remember putting June Sarpong and Margherita Taylor together to present a show when I was in charge of *T4* – I just thought they were great presenters; I hadn't considered that they were also two women of colour. They both spoke to me about it because they felt that it was a breakthrough moment for them to present a major entertainment show on Channel 4 together. It's not why I had decided to give them the jobs, but even so, the fact that they were heading up the show was big.

I don't believe in 'tokenism'. I think that putting someone on TV who isn't ready for that role is unfair on the person presenting – they shouldn't be put in a position like that just because it makes TV companies and channels look good. It's important that when someone is given a role, they're on there for the right reasons, and we have to start casting the net further when we look for people to be on television. But I don't believe someone should be put on TV just because of the colour of their skin. Representation has to improve, but in the right way, and not just to tick a box.

You've had an incredibly varied and interesting career, but is there a dream job that you'd love to do?

My dream job is probably a daily magazine show – like *Oprah* but called Andi! I sat in for Lorraine Kelly on her show recently and loved every minute of it. Having a daily show where everyone tunes in to watch me chatting to celebrities or talking about what's going on in the world would be my absolute dream.

What is the one piece of advice you'd give to aspiring presenters, or any readers wanting to get into the TV industry? Have you got a top tip?

It's really quite simple. Don't give up. Believe in yourself. Be the best. My parents always told me that, as a Black kid, I'd have to work harder to prove myself. And although it shouldn't be this way, I believe it's still true. You do have to work that extra bit harder to make sure you're noticed, respected and that people realize that you're great at what you do. TV is very competitive, so the very best piece of advice I can give is to always try and be better than the person next to you, and to make sure you stand out from the crowd.

SARAH FORBES BONETTA

ELEGANT SOCIETY PRINCESS

WHO WAS SHE? An Egbado princess who was orphaned and forced into slavery at the age of five. Sarah was taken to England and became a hit in society circles.

WHEN WAS SHE AROUND? 1843–1880

WHY IS SHE IMPORTANT? Sarah so impressed Queen Victoria when they met that the queen decided to take the role of Sarah's godmother. At a time when Black people were seen as lesser than white people, this was a big deal and broke boundaries!

Sarah's story is such an astonishing one. She was born in West Africa (south-west Nigeria today) as **Aina, the daughter of Yoruba royalty**. When she was young, her parents were killed during a war, and Sarah was captured by King Ghezo of Dahomey (now Benin), an infamous slave trader.

Captain Frederick Forbes, a British Royal Navy officer, was visiting Dahomey in 1849. He was sent there on a diplomatic mission to try and persuade King Ghezo to give up his involvement in the Atlantic slave trade on the grounds that it was morally wrong. Remember, parts of Africa were under **BRITISH COLONIAL RULE** at this time.

QUICK FACTS: COLONIZATION

The British colonized Africa around 1870. Africa had a wealth of resources, including gold, ivory, salt and rubber. Britain wanted resources like this to use in manufacturing. Britain ruled over many countries, including what's now known as Sudan, Kenya, Botswana, Egypt, Gambia and Nigeria.

The British governed by what's called 'indirect rule'. This means that they controlled the countries by making African tribal leaders do the work they wanted them to, rather than having people from Britain running the countries. This was different to some other parts of the empire where the British worked, lived and ruled directly. As you can imagine, not everyone was happy with this way of living, or the idea of being controlled by a country far away. Many wars and rebellions happened, and Britain often had to send soldiers to enforce their rules.

Dahomey wasn't a British colony. It was ruled by France (King Ghezo had freed Dahomey after defeating the Oyo Empire in 1823). They made a lot of money from having slaves, so he wasn't going to ever agree to not being part of the slave trade.

While he was there, somehow, Captain Forbes managed to get Aina released into his care so that he was responsible for her. We're not totally sure how this happened, but some people reckon that Aina was suggested as a 'diplomatic gift', with Frederick telling the king how she'd make a good present for Queen Victoria. The very idea of giving her from one royal to another would have no doubt pleased King Ghezo, who'd have viewed this as a positive political move. It sounds pretty awful that a person could be given away like this, but it did mean that Sarah was able to escape from the king.

So, even though I don't like at all the idea of people being thought of as objects that could be given away, I'm going to give Forbes the benefit of the doubt that he did it to help Sarah have a much better life away from this tyrant king!

In July 1850, when she was around seven years old, Captain Forbes brought Aina over to England. It was at this point that she became known as Sarah Forbes Bonetta, which was a combination of the captain's own name and the name of his ship. As I've said before, it wasn't uncommon for enslaved people to be renamed in this way, although I'm sure it would have been confusing for a seven-year-old to suddenly be on her way to a new country with a brand-new name.

In his journals and memoirs, Captain Forbes writes about meeting her:

'For her age supposed to be eight years. She is a perfect genius; she now speaks English well, and has a great talent for music. She has won the affections, with but few exceptions, of all who have known her, she is far in advance of any white child of her age, in aptness of learning, and strength of mind and affection.'

On arriving back in England, Forbes introduced Sarah to Queen Victoria, who was very impressed, and her impressions of Sarah when they first met can be found in her diaries:

> 'When we came home, found Albert still there, waiting for Capt: Forbes & a poor little ... girl, whom he brought back from the King of Dahomé, her Parents & all her relatives having been sacrificed. Capt: Forbes saved her life, by asking for her as a present ... She is 7 years old, sharp & intelligent, & speaks English.'

From these descriptions it's clear that from a young age Sarah was starting to challenge some of the narrow-minded views and stereotypes that people believed about African people at the time.

Queen Victoria made sure that Sarah had a decent education by sending her for schooling with the Church Missionary Society. Some people wonder why the queen helped her, but many have suggested that Queen Victoria might have felt sorry for her since she was an orphan. Plus, Sarah's own family had been Yoruba royalty, so perhaps the queen felt linked to the small girl in that way? From what we know, Queen Victoria was definitely impressed by Sarah's intelligence.

Perhaps affected by the cold English climate, Sarah spent much of her first year in Britain feeling quite poorly. So, in 1851, she was sent back to Africa to go to school in Sierra Leone, where it was thought it would be a better climate for her health.

Once Sarah was twelve, Queen Victoria asked for her to come back to England and to be looked after by a couple in Chatham, Kent, called Mr and Mrs Schoen. The queen gave Sarah money towards her upbringing, and Sarah visited Windsor Castle loads, too.

When she was eighteen, she got a marriage proposal from James Pinson Labulo Davies, a wealthy Yoruba businessman living in Britain. He'd been liberated from a slave ship by the Royal Navy and was thirty-one years old. Sarah was clearly enjoying being a free woman because, at first, she really didn't want to marry him. She wrote to Mrs Schoen:

'Others would say "He is a good man & though you don't care about him now, will soon learn to love him." That, I believe, I never could do. I know that the generality of people would say he is rich & your marrying him would at once make you independent, and I say "Am I to barter my peace of mind for money?" No — never!'

She sounds so certain, like no one could change her mind, but change her mind she did! They got married in August 1862 in Brighton. **Sarah wrote her birth name on her marriage certificate – Aina. I love this – she reclaims her own identity by using the name taken from her. At a huge moment in her life, she chose to make a big statement.** I'm going to follow her lead and use her real name from now on, cos this part of her life is purely Aina's.

Once Aina and James got married they moved back to West Africa and lived in Lagos, Nigeria. Aina had their first daughter soon after. She asked the queen's permission to name her daughter Victoria. The queen agreed and also became Aina's daughter's godmother!

Aina brought her daughter to visit Queen Victoria in 1867 and then went back to Lagos, where she had two more children.

Queen Victoria obviously had a real soft spot for Aina and her family, and when her daughter passed her music exams, the queen gave the general public a day's holiday!

In 1880, after suffering from tuberculosis, Aina travelled to Madeira to rest, but she died around the age of forty and was buried in Funchal, Madeira. Queen Victoria wrote about her death in her diary:

'Saw poor Victoria Davies, my black godchild, who learnt this morning of the death of her dear mother'.

Even after Aina's death, her family remained important to Queen Victoria as she continued giving an allowance to Victoria, who often visited the royal household during her lifetime.

Sarah's life was pretty extraordinary, which is why it's made it into the history books - although I was never told about her at school!

What I find really interesting is how it shows some Victorians had different attitudes about race. It's wonderful that she was recognized, not just by the queen, but by others too, as being intelligent and capable. She stopped any negative stereotypes in their tracks, and clearly the queen was very fond of her!

But we should also consider that perhaps it was moving to cold Britain that affected her health badly, and, although she might have had a better life here, who knows if she might have lived longer if she'd been allowed to live safely and happily in her own country.

THE TWENTIETH CENTURY

Wow, we've reached the twentieth century – now that sounds a bit more modern, doesn't it? This was a time of massive leaps forward in technology, amazing discoveries and inventions, and even humankind's first steps into space exploration! But as well as all those amazing things, the globe was also dominated by two world wars, in the first half of the century and then continued political tensions for the next fifty years – a lot of which we're still feeling the impact of today.

When it came to race relations, the twentieth century does feel like a turning point. There was still a huge amount of racism in society, but things were changing – well, people were making it change, with protests and civil unrest as they stood up to make a difference and to ensure their voices were heard.

We often think of the American civil rights movement and amazing people like Martin Luther

King Jr. when we talk about protesting racism and inequality, but as we've seen during our journey into the more-distant past, there have always been incredible people here in Britain speaking up, creating change and never letting prejudice hold them back . . . Let's meet them! Starting with the Tull Brothers.

Now, here's something exciting – **a two-for-one deal!** Two brothers, both trailblazers in different fields: one a sportsman and war hero, the other an academic and dentist. They must have had to deal with bad attitudes and racism, but they both carried on doing awesome things. They refused to let anything or anyone hold them back. And I really love this attitude! Do you want to know more? Well, that's good, because I'm excited to tell you their stories.

WALTER TULL

HERO ON AND OFF THE FOOTBALL PITCH

WHO WAS HE? One of the first Black professional footballers in Britain, and a war hero.

WHEN WAS HE AROUND? 1888–1918

WHY IS HE IMPORTANT? Walter Tull broke the mould when it came to football, becoming one of the first Black professional players and signing for Clapton, Tottenham Hotspur, Northampton Town and Rangers FC. When the First World War broke out, Walter served as a soldier on the front lines and was sadly killed in action in 1918.

Walter Tull's story is one that really moves me, I think partly because I've got a son, and partly because I know that brilliant superstars like Marcus Rashford, Raheem Sterling and others – who do so much good in our world – still receive horrendous abuse on the pitch.

It can seem like very little progress has been made in the fight against racism and ignorance. Really, we should all know better by now! But looking at history can teach us what to do better in the here and now, which is why we have to talk about these heroes and tell these people's stories. We have to make sure that we do our school projects about them, and that they don't go forgotten in our history books for the next hundred years. Who's with me? Good!

So, back to Walter! Walter Tull was born in Folkstone, Kent, on 28 April 1888. His father, Daniel Tull, came over from Barbados because he didn't like the way he was being treated over there. Walter's mum was local, from Kent. So, Walter and his siblings were mixed race.

Sadly, when Walter was just seven years old, his mum died and his dad remarried. Then, in 1897, his dad died too, and Walter, now only nine years old, was sent to Wesleyan Methodist Children's Home in Lambeth, London, along with his older brother, Edward.

Can you imagine how completely different that must have been to what they'd been used to? I like to think that they might have seen more Black and brown faces around, as Lambeth was probably way more diverse than Folkstone!

Research tells us that Walter adapted all right to life in the orphanage, maybe because he was young. But Edward found it a bit of a struggle. The orphanage was known for being into music and worship, and Walter and his brother joined a choir and they used to tour to fundraise.

It was on one of these tours that Edward got spotted by a couple from Glasgow who wanted to adopt him.

I'll tell you more about Edward's life in a minute!

That meant that Walter

was all on his own, the poor lad! In just a few years he'd gone from living with a big family to being alone. Maybe that's why he

Can you imagine being separated from your siblings like that?

threw himself into the one thing he clearly loved: playing football. And he was good, too! **It didn't take long before he was taken on by Clapton FC and started training and playing for them.**

It was when he was playing for Clapton FC that Walter was spotted and signed by Tottenham Hotspur FC. He starting playing for Tottenham in 1909 and was only the second Black man to play in a football league's top division – Walter played for them for two years before moving on to play for Northampton Town FC, where he

Isn't that outrageous?

scored over a hundred goals! That's about the same as Peter Crouch or Ian Wright scored in their whole Premier League careers (as some football buff told me!).

Although there are many Black and international players now, a hundred years ago, when Walter was seen regularly on the pitch, some crowds didn't like it. People said racist things about him in the newspapers. Honestly, it broke my heart to read some of the names he was called and the disgusting words used. I won't repeat them here, but I do know that Black footballers today are often treated in the same negative way and it's just not on.

When will things change?!

Despite the abuse he faced, Walter continued to play, but just as he was getting into his brilliant football career, the First World War broke out in Europe. England encouraged its young men to sign up to fight for their country and that meant that professional football was put on hold.

On 21 December 1914, Walter left Northampton and went to the army recruitment office. But they weren't keen on Black people at all. The 1914 edition *of The Manual of Military Law* tells us loud and clear exactly what their feelings were:

> 'troops formed of coloured individuals belonging to savage tribes and barbarous races should not be employed in a war between civilised states.'

Just look at the language used here! To think that Britain, a country I'm proud to be a part of, was so racist and narrow-minded as to refer to Black and brown people as 'savage tribes and barbarous races' when they had no idea or regard for the folks that had actually been born over here. It's important to remember, though, that lots of these people had never met any Black people or received any education, which must have contributed to these ill-informed attitudes.

Like lots of the other people in this book, Walter wasn't one to take no for an answer, so, ignoring the rules, he signed up to join the first Footballers' Battalion, which was a troop of about a thousand men. The army hoped that if professional footballers signed up, it would encourage young men who were football fans to also sign up, as these young, fit, and healthy men were exactly who the government wanted fighting.

Walter trained as a lance corporal and, in November 1915, he finished his basic training and boarded a ship to France for war.

I can't begin to think about what experiencing a war would have been like for young men like Walter. Imagine being confronted with death, injury and violence, as well as leaving your family and living in appallingly harsh conditions. It's well-documented that there were rats in the trenches and the weather could be terrible, with no home comforts or enough food to eat. In 1915, after serving the army in France and witnessing the horrors on the battlefield, poor Walter was sent to hospital for **SHELL SHOCK**.

QUICK FACTS: SHELL SHOCK

During the First World War many soldiers came back from the trenches deaf, blind, mute or paralysed. No one knew what was wrong with them as they hadn't been otherwise injured during the fighting.

Then, in 1917, Charles Myers, a medical officer, first used the term 'shell shock'. Today we'd call it post-traumatic stress disorder (PTSD).

There were deep consequences to being in and around a war zone. Even if soldiers hadn't seen any direct action on the front lines, hearing all the bombs, seeing the wounded and just being in such an extraordinary situation really affected them mentally and physically.

Often, the soldiers who were shell-shocked couldn't eat or sleep, and some developed physical symptoms, too. Given what a scary and strange thing fighting in a war must have been for young men, it's not surprising it impacted them so severely, is it?

But the army needed all the soldiers they could get, so Walter had to come back to active duty in September 1916. Then he fought at the **Battle of the Somme**, a big battle that took place in France.

Despite those racist rules we read above which meant he wasn't supposed to be commissioned as an officer, **Walter did get rewarded for his contributions and was promoted to lieutenant in 1917. He was the first Black man to become an infantry officer in the British army, so yet again he was breaking the mould of what was expected of Black people at the time.**

Here's where I would love to tell you that Walter returned home a hero and got back on the football pitch doing what he loved. But sadly, Walter's story doesn't have a happy ending. **He was killed in action in March 1918**, aged just twenty-nine. But consider how many barriers this man broke through in his too-short life.

According to the government's National Archives, Britain lost some 886,000 troops during the First World War. Think of all those lives wiped out...

Walter was recommended by the commanding officer of the 23rd Battalion to receive a Military Cross for bravery, but sadly, he hasn't been issued with one yet. Many people think this is because Walter was Black, and as the British army didn't officially commission Black soldiers, they couldn't issue them medals.

Nevertheless, people have continued to campaign for Walter to receive the medal he deserves. And it isn't just Walter who has been denied recognition; the same is sadly true for thousands of Black and Asian troops. In April 2021, the UK Prime Minister Boris Johnson spoke of being 'deeply troubled' by the fact that so many people have never been properly honoured for

I really hope so.

their brave actions during the First World War. Whether or not medals will ever be given is another matter.

To be honest with you, even though I'm usually full of laughs and smiles, discovering this has upset me. But, rather than staying sad, I think it's time to sort this out! So, how can we change this? We can ask about these people. We can create petitions. It has worked in the past. For instance, back in 2013, over 36,000 signatures from a petition organized by Operation Black Vote meant that both **Mary Seacole** and **Olaudah Equiano** weren't taken off the school curriculum.

Walter might not have the medal, but he does have a bronze statue in the courtyard at the Guildhall, Northampton. In 2014, he was also honoured with an English Heritage blue plaque in Tottenham, where he played, and there is also a memorial at Sixfields Stadium in Northampton, where he played before the war.

So we can be sure that, medal or no medal, people won't forget Walter, his amazing footie skills or his war heroics.

AMAZING HERE AND NOW
JERMAINE JENAS

JERMAINE JENAS *started his professional football career at Nottingham Forest when he was just 17, and then went on to play for loads of amazing top level clubs, including Tottenham Hotspur – just like Walter Tull! – and for England, too! Now he's ALL OVER our TV screens, not only as a football pundit, but also presenting prime-time telly and hard-hitting documentaries. I'm SO impressed by how Jermaine has used his profile to speak out about racism in football and beyond, making him a superstar both on the pitch and off! Let's find out more about him!*

You started out as a footballer at a pretty young age and even played for the England under-15 team. What's it like setting out on a career path so early? Did you ever want to be anything other than a professional football player?

Football was my first love – the first thing I felt passionate about, if I'm honest. I didn't realise it could be a career for me probably until I got to the age of 15, when everyone at school was talking about collage and university. I was just thinking about running and getting fit – my university was the football pitch.

There's another layer to all of it, though. My dad was a coach and taught me how to play football, but he was very demanding. I remember games when I was, like, 9, and I'd play well and score four goals and I'd come off the pitch happy, but my dad would still pick my game apart – what I didn't do or what I should have done better. But actually I love him for doing that and always pushing me to be my best. Thank God that he was so driven to helping me achieve my goal!

When my parents separated, things definitely got tougher at home for me. My mum was solid, though, and would always piece me back together. That's another reason why football and becoming a footballer was all I ever wanted – I knew it would make my mum's life better if I were successful.

It's amazing that you not only played in the Premier League but also represented England internationally! Is there a very different pressure playing on an international stage compared to a club?

I was lucky that I played for and was involved in England teams and the set-up of international football for the under-15s all the way to first-team level. I also captained most of these teams which gave me a sense of authority and belonging. The pressure of playing internationally is very different. With your club only your fans want you to do well, but playing for your country, the whole of England expects it! You always feel the pressure, I think. The World Cup in 2006 was where I saw it and felt it most. I didn't play, which was disappointing, but I observed a lot of what was going on and the pressure was intense.

I've just been sharing Walter Tull's story and legacy in football. As one of the first Black men to be a professional footballer in England, he received lots of racist abuse despite being an amazing player. Even now, football is still battling to combat racism. What do you think of the fact that players today are still facing the same abuse as Walter did, over 100 years ago?

Growing up, racism was a big topic and one that we spoke about a lot in my house. We lived in a predominantly white area and my mum was with a Black man. I heard the N— word daily. Some of the incidents really stuck with me, for example I remember once I kicked a football over into the next door garden, I snuck in to get it and the old man who lived there just opened the window and swore and shouted racist abuse at me. I was so upset that an adult could think it was OK to speak to me like that! But what he didn't know (and quickly found out!) is you don't mess with my mum's son!

When it comes to football, the fans within the stadium and across the country have always been a big representation of our society in England, so it does surprise me that racism is still as bad now as it was for Walter Tull. We like to think that as a country we've improved and become less bigoted. My opinion is that people have gone from just shouting it out the window to someone's son to just inwardly thinking it or creating a fake social media account and expressing what they really want to shout on there.

Walter played for Tottenham Hotspur, just like you! Were you aware of him when you were there? What do you think of his story?

Walter Tull's story is amazing and I was made aware of him when I was playing for Tottenham because of his role at the club. Walter was a leader on the pitch and then in his position within the Army. I remember being in awe of him and what he managed to do. It was so disappointing that I wasn't taught anything about people like Walter Tull and their history at school, but I'm glad that with books like this his story is getting shared as it should!

Have you been inspired by any other footballers or sportspeople? If you could meet any player from the past (or now!) who would it be and why?

John Barnes was my hero as a kid and the only player I ever wanted to meet. I had a video tape about him called *The John Barnes Story* and I watched it every day. In my house, John Barnes was like a god! A Black man who came to England from Jamaica and was too good for them all! A man who played with a smile on his face when people were throwing bananas at him. Everything about John as a player inspired me and helped to shape me, not only with the drive and determination to become a footballer but also on how to deal with hate. I had the chance to meet and work with him after I retired, and he didn't disappoint at all. Legend.

Now that you're retired from professional football, you're using your platform to discuss big issues like online trolling, knife crime and racism in sport, which is just amazing, as voices like yours can really help to drive change. What is your advice to the young activists reading this book who want to make a difference, like you?

This is a difficult question to answer as I feel all of these feelings and thoughts on social issues come from within. I've always felt I have a responsibility, almost a duty, to use my voice and my platform. I think a lot of it stems back to my youth and the values and principles that my parents instilled in me.

My advice, though, is if a subject creates an emotion in you – anger, sadness, whatever it may be – then it's worth investigating to find out more. That's definitely why I've been involved in the documentaries I've done for TV; I'll investigate, read about it, have conversations with people and try and get a feeling for the subject. If, at the end of all that I'm still angry, still fired up, then I know it's time to go and make the programme and share my message.

So, if anyone reading this wants to speak up, about anything, then I say go for it!

EDWARD TULL-WARNOCK

DENTAL PIONEER

WHO WAS HE? Potentially the first ever professional Black dentist in Britain.

WHEN WAS HE AROUND? 1886–1950

WHY IS HE IMPORTANT? Like his trailblazing brother, Edward worked his way up to the top of his career, smashing stereotypes as he strove for success!

Walter's brother has his own extraordinary story, too! **Edward, born in 1886, was two years older than Walter.** As we've learned, at the children's home in Lambeth, the boys were part of a choir. During a performance, Jeanie and James Warnock from Glasgow decided they wanted to adopt Edward. It seems like they had real heart; they'd both had their own hard experiences of orphanages and poverty themselves growing up, so perhaps they wanted to help other children have good lives.

Jeanie's brother was a dentist and James, her husband, had given up his printing job to retrain as a dentist himself. After the adoption Jeanie and James sent Edward to one of the best schools 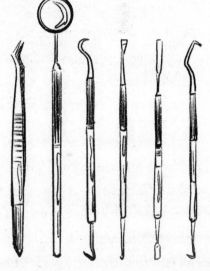 in Glasgow, and he did really well. **He was a clever boy and went on to become one of (we think!) the first ever professional Black dentists in Britain.** They are not many records of dentists from a non-white background, so we'll never know for sure if he was the *first*, but it doesn't really matter – he was still forging a path for other Black dentists in his wake.

For so long, people had looked for proof that Black people were morally and intellectually inferior. If people had known how clever Edward was, it would have blown their minds! Edward's tutors described him as:

> '[taking] painstaking zeal in his work . . . took second place for the Dall and Ash prizes for 1909 . . . the former [prize] for the . . . highest marks . . . in operative work, and the latter [prize being] for the best all-round record . . . Mr Warnock is gentlemanly, courteous, and obliging.'

Edward joined the Glasgow Dental Hospital in 1906 and graduated in 1910. Over his career, he went on to become a member of the Royal College of Physicians and Surgeons in Glasgow, and won prizes for the work he did. I'd have definitely let him work his magic on my choppers!

Just like his brother, Edward's career choice meant that he openly encountered racism because he was one of the only Black people in the profession and people didn't think he could

be as good as the white people he worked alongside.

We know that when he went for his first job in 1910 in Birmingham, and although he'd already sent a picture of himself to his employer (maybe hoping to avoid any issues), when they met the man said: 'My God, you're coloured! You'll destroy my practice in twenty-four hours!'

Can you believe that?!

Not wanting to give up (a family trait it seems!), Edward took all his quality training and went to work with his dad in Glasgow and, later, in Aberdeen. That's where he met his wife.

We don't know much about Edward's working life, but there *is* a record of him writing in support of the Dentists Act in 1921. This was a law which wanted to make sure that dentists practising were properly trained with qualifications.

Apparently, up until then, people could just say they knew what they were doing even if they didn't! I mean, thank goodness we had people like Edward on the case! In his letter, he said:

> 'The qualified dentist of the present day has a good chance of raising the dental profession to the level of the medical for the future.'

. . . which shows he was not only proud of his job, but was also someone who always looked forward and pushed for change. Not surprising, given that as a Black man, just the fact he *was* a trained dentist was a change to the traditional expectations.

Even though Edward and Walter were separated – one brother living in Glasgow and one in Lambeth – Edward's adoptive family made sure they kept in contact with Walter, and he was invited up to see them, so the brothers stayed in touch.

Some of you might have heard of Walter before this book, but I bet you had no idea he had a brother who also blazed a trail for Black people in Britain? Edward's story definitely isn't as widely shared as Walter's. It makes you think, doesn't it, about which narratives we're given throughout history.

Why is Walter more well-known? I wonder if it's because sport and war are seen as more British, traditional or exciting? Perhaps people are more comfortable emphasizing sportsmanship and teamwork (so, war and sport) over academic achievement (dentistry). I bet that if anyone was choosing between the two, then they'd definitely see football as more glam than pulling someone's teeth out, right? But the truth is that both boys excelled in their areas; they were focused and determined to succeed despite the hurdles they both had to clear.

I wonder who inspired them as they took their trailblazing steps to become the only Black people in professions that were seen as only appropriate for white people?

LILIAN BADER

CLEVER CORPORAL

WHO WAS SHE? One of the first Black women who joined the Royal Air Force.

WHEN WAS SHE AROUND? 1918–2015

WHY IS SHE IMPORTANT? At a time when Black people weren't allowed to join the British armed forces, Lilian was determined to serve her country and found a way around the rules. Like many women in the Second World War, she also pushed gender boundaries by taking on a 'man's job' and smashing it!

Lilian was born in 1918, in Liverpool. Her dad was of Barbadian heritage and her mum was Irish. Sadly, her parents died when Lilian was only nine years old and then she got sent to a convent. No one would give her work as she got older because of her race, and so she had to stay in the convent until she was twenty.

I'm not sure what changed for her, but eventually, in Yorkshire, Lilian got a job at a Navy, Army and Air Force Institute canteen. It seems that she might have got the job because Lilian's lighter skin meant people didn't realize at first that she wasn't white, but when her dad's West Indian heritage was discovered, Lilian was made to leave her job! This was because there was something called a **COLOUR BAR** in the armed forces at this time.

QUICK FACTS: THE COLOUR BAR

A colour bar is when a system is in place where people of different races are separated and not given the same rights and opportunities. Here we're talking about the colour bar in the British Military but there are other organizations who enforced similar rules.

Walter Tull was refused entry to the British army in 1914, but in 1939, a few weeks after the Second World War had been declared, the colour bar in place at the time was lifted. Perhaps they'd learned from the First World War?! You'd hope so, right?

The Royal Navy and Army didn't rush to allow Black officers to sign up, but the Air Force did get on to it and recruited. Many volunteers from the Caribbean joined the Royal Air Force, where they felt most welcome. The old colour bar from the First World War said only men of 'pure European descent' could fight. Ridiculous, right? There were some exceptions for the RAF, but even there, being promoted to the rank of officer wasn't allowed. The colour bar did eventually get lifted completely in 1947, after the end of the Second World War, but even then, this racism didn't suddenly vanish. And yet, over 6,000 people from the Caribbean served in the Second World War.

In the 1940s, the RAF started to recruit volunteers who were from the Caribbean. Lilian heard a group of West Indians speak on the radio. They'd been told they couldn't join the army because of the colour bar but they had managed to successfully join the RAF. This was music to Lilian's ears and, in **1941, she enlisted with the Women's Auxiliary Air Force (WAAF).**

She said that she found herself

> *'the only coloured person in this sea of white faces, but somebody told me I looked smart in my uniform, which cheered me no end.'*

Lilian trained as an instrument repairer, which was a new trade for women. She went to work at

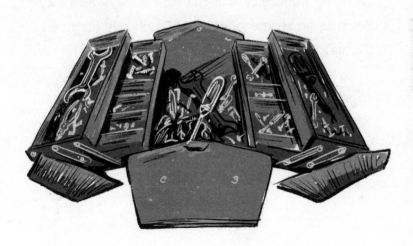

RAF Shawbury in Shropshire at the end of 1941, checking the instruments of the aircrafts for faults. It was a really important job! While she was there, she impressed those at the top and was given the rank of acting corporal.

Nice one, Lilian!

Lilian married Ramsay Bader in 1943. Ramsay was also a serviceman and mixed race, so they must have had a lot in common. Lilian became pregnant in 1944 and was discharged from the WAAF. She went on to have two sons.

After the war had finished, Lilian did a degree at London University and had a career as a teacher, which she carried on doing until she was in her eighties. Her younger son grew up to fly helicopters in the Royal Navy and later became an airline pilot! So she clearly inspired the next generation, which is fantastic to know.

In 1989, Lilian wrote a book about her life called *Together – Lilian Bader: Wartime Memoirs of a WAAF 1939–1944*. In it, she said:

'Father served in the First World War, his three children served in the Second World War. I married a coloured man who was in the Second World War, as was his brother who was decorated for bravery in Burma. Their father also served in the First World War. Our son was a helicopter pilot, he served in Northern Ireland. So all in all, I think we've given back more to this country than we've received.'

Her words hit pretty hard, I think. Sounds like quite a family, all stepping up and putting themselves in danger for a country that for the most part couldn't see beyond the colour of their skin. **Lilian speaks for many who made sacrifices during the two world wars, and I'm glad that things have changed and now we are beginning to recognize the contribution of all those who fought so bravely!**

Lilian died in March 2015, aged 97.

CONNIE MARK

CELEBRATED CAMPAIGNER

WHO WAS SHE? An activist who campaigned for the recognition of Black service personnel.

WHEN WAS SHE AROUND? 1923–2007

WHY IS SHE IMPORTANT? Connie Mark dedicated so much of her life to making sure that the contribution of Black people in military service was recognized and celebrated. She received two medals from Queen Elizabeth for her activism and hard work.

Connie Mark was born on 21 December 1923 in Kingston, Jamaica. It sounds like she had a great time as a kid, spending lots of happy Sundays at church with her friends and family – religion was really important to her. She also played the piano and enjoyed going swimming before school.

Connie was just sixteen when the Second World War was announced. At this time, Jamaica was still under British colonial rule, and **in 1943, Connie served in the Auxiliary Territorial Service (ATS), which was the women's side of the British army during the war.** She also worked in the British military hospital in Kingston, where her job was as a medical secretary – she used to have to write up accounts of all the injuries the soldiers had suffered.

Eww, bet she must have had a strong stomach not to be affected by all of that!

Connie was a good worker and was promoted through the ranks really quickly. After just six months as a private (where everyone starts as a beginner), she was made lance corporal (the boss), and then another six months after that, a corporal (a BIGGER boss!). These promotions sound great but, shamefully, she didn't receive any more money! Apparently, the War Office said that women in the

ATS weren't entitled to pay rises even if they took on higher-level jobs.

When the war was over, Connie's boss recommended she was awarded the British Empire Medal to acknowledge her fantastic service, but she didn't get it. Connie thought that she was refused the medal because of racism, and because she refused to clean the rooms of British officers during the war.

I mean, why she should she have done that? Those men should have learned how to clean up after themselves!

Connie married a guy called Stanley Goodridge in 1952 and they had a daughter, Amru Elizabeth. Stanley was a fast cricket bowler and the whole family moved to Britain when he was offered a job at a cricket club there. In 1957, Connie had a little boy, Stanley.

Connie said in an interview how she remembers the accommodation in Britain being so small:

'You come here and are stuck in one room with a husband and a baby . . . that was the biggest shock for me because nobody told me or warned me!'

I'm guessing that the size of her flat wasn't the only thing that shocked Connie. I mean, can you imagine living behind the lovely sunshine of Jamaica for the gloom and rain of Britain?! Plus, as we know from the other people in this book, there were lots of people with bad attitudes towards race at this time. Connie said at first she had problems getting work, with employers making excuses about her qualifications as a way to get rid of her. Some of that would likely have been because she was a Black woman.

But she never gave up, and eventually she found work as a medical secretary and got back to doing what she knew best. She also became involved in community projects and working with various charities. One of these was the **West Indian Ex-Servicemen's Association**, which had formed after the war so West Indian people who had fought for Britain could support each other. As someone who was passionate about equality, it's no surprise that Connie joined – and then campaigned for the organization to add women to their title! Nice one!

A few years later, Connie and Stanley got divorced, and she married another man called Michael Mark.

In 1980, Connie founded Friends of Mary Seacole (which is now called the Mary Seacole Memorial Association), so just like me, she clearly thought that Mary was an awesome lady who deserved to be remembered! I think she probably felt like she totally related to Mary's story. After all, even though the Second World War was nearly a hundred years after the Crimean War, Connie's contribution (like Mary's) was overlooked and ignored by those in charge! Connie also campaigned for the efforts of Caribbean people during the war to be remembered.

Here's the part of Connie's story that I'm really happy about – remember that medal she wasn't awarded? Well, **in 1992, Connie finally got given the British Empire Medal for her service during the war.**

I was glad to see this since she'd worked for the British military for over a decade!

Plus, unlike so many other people in this book, Connie actually got to receive her award while she was alive. I bet she was so proud on that day.

And then there was more good news to come because, in 1993, the British government created a bursary fund honouring Mary Seacole, and started giving £25,000 every year towards nursing leadership studies. This news must have been music to Connie's ears, since she'd been working to get Mary Seacole some recognition for thirteen years!

ETHEL SCOTT

SENSATIONAL SPRINTER

WHO WAS SHE? The first Black women to represent Great Britain in international athletics.

WHEN WAS SHE AROUND? 1907–1984

WHY IS SHE IMPORTANT? Ethel took part in several international competitions in the 1930s. Before this point, not a single Black woman had ever been selected to compete in this way, so she literally ran a blazing trail!

Ethel Scott is someone that we don't have loads of information on at all, but from the little I do know, she sounds like a wonderful, strong woman, who we *should* all know about, so I'm going to tell you what I can! It's pretty interesting to think about how, of the women we have mentioned so far, three of them had to write their own account of their own lives!

It's a good job those women *did* write about their lives, or even more stories might have been lost to history! We know that men and their achievements were always considered more important than women . . . and being a Black woman almost gave you double invisibility, which is not as cool a superpower as it sounds when it comes to the history books!

Anyway, **Ethel was a sprinter and short-distance runner.** The 60m sprint and the 400m relay were what she was best at, so she could have given women like Denise Lewis, Dina Asher-Smith and Christine Ohuruogu a run for their money.

Ha - 'run'!
Do you like what
I did there?!

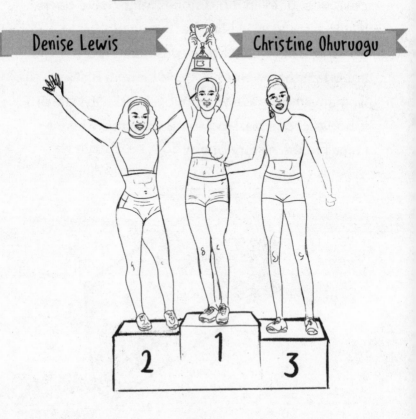

Dina Asher-Smith

Denise Lewis

Christine Ohuruogu

2

1

3

There's evidence that Ethel competed between 1928 and 1950, so she must have been good to have been in competitive sport for a while.

Ethel set a personal best for the 60m sprint in August 1930 in Mitcham, London. She did the race in 7.8 seconds; this was just off the world record, which was 7.6 seconds back then. But it matched the British record at the time, which had been set by a women called Mary Lins in 1922.

There's a brilliant picture of Ethel that I came across during my research where she's standing, proud as anything, surrounded by loads of medals and cups and prizes (one of them is a tea set!). I found it almost unbelievable.

Google it!

Of course, now we have loads of Black British athletes (thank goodness!), but not much is known about women's athletics back in those days, let alone Black women's athletics, so that picture is a fantastic piece of evidence about Ethel's life. They say a picture is worth a thousand words, so even though what we know about Ethel is so small, I think this picture says a lot!

You go, girl!

AMAZING HERE AND NOW
DINA ASHER-SMITH

DINA ASHER-SMITH *is currently the fastest British woman in history (wow!) and holds British records in the 100-metres, 200-metres and 4 x 100-metres events. She represented Team GB at the 2016 and 2020 Olympics, winning medals at both games. I'm just glad that she managed to slow down enough to answer some of my questions, because there's no way I could have caught her on the running track!*

What age were you when you first started athletics? Did you always know you wanted to be a competitive athlete?

I began running when I was eight years old, and I think being a competitive athlete was my first serious aspiration. I wanted to be a lot of things when I was younger, but I remember thinking when I watched the Athens Olympics in 2004 that the whole idea of going to the Olympic Games was great. And it was then that I decided I wanted to be an Olympian. I didn't quite know what sport, but I wanted to go to the Olympics.

You've broken SO many records across your career, but what's been your proudest achievement?

The proudest achievement of my career would have to be becoming World Champion, which is obviously amazing, but I do also recall that going sub-22 seconds for the 200-metre made me feel really proud. Obviously, everything is hard, but that achievement, physically, in terms of the training, is a very difficult feat. I was really happy to have been able to run sub-22, and then run sub-22 more than once. Hopefully I'll remain a sub-22-second sprinter for a really long time.

We've just learned about Ethel Scott, an amazing Black woman who represented her country at an international level, just like you. But before researching this book, I'd never heard of her! Had you heard of Ethel before? What do you think about her story?

I hadn't heard of Ethel Scott before, and I think that says a lot in itself! I think her achievements are absolutely amazing. Especially to have been running in the 1930s, when technology was different, tracks were different, equipment was different – that was incredibly fast running. I think she was brilliant, and it would have been great to have known more about her, but I guess that is exactly what this book aims to do!

What would your best piece of advice be to anyone reading this, who wants to follow in yours and Ethel's (very fast!) footsteps?

My piece of advice would be to just go for it. Life is short and you might as well pursue everything that you want to do. That's important, but also remember to work hard and be patient. Sport has shown me that you can't just train one day and be incredible and world class immediately the day after. You must work consistently hard and dedicate yourself, and that means sleeping right and eating right, and doing all the things that might seem inconsequential or quite small on the outside, but they really do add up and make a big difference. So, my main advice is to go for it and make sure you're having fun.

This book is all about showcasing amazing Black people throughout our history. Is there a famous (or not so famous) Black person who's inspired you?

Yes, there are loads and loads and loads of people who have inspired me. Christine Ohuruogu is one of my incredible inspirations. To name a few more: Jessica Ennis-Hill, Allyson Felix, Serena Williams; there have been many. I am very fortunate to have grown up when there were loads of incredible Black women doing amazing things, particularly in my sport, and in the UK.

In your opinion, do you think I have what it takes to be an athlete?

I think you do. I think everybody has what it takes to be an athlete, simply because we are all athletes. All you need to do is pick something, get started and go out there and enjoy it. So yeah, go for it, take your pick of whatever you'd like to do!

FACT FILE: THE WINDRUSH GENERATION

On 22 June 1948, around five hundred people from the Caribbean arrived at Tilbury Docks in Essex on a boat called the SS *Empire Windrush*.

EMPIRE WINDRUSH

Why would people leave their country and their homes in the Caribbean, you might ask? Well, Britain needed help to recover from all the damage of the Second World War. Buildings had been bombed, houses had been destroyed and everything needed to be rebuilt. People answered adverts to come and help – there was work to be done, jobs to be had. So, they boarded the SS *Empire Windrush* and travelled thousands of miles across the Atlantic Ocean to Britain.

The arrival of the SS *Empire Windrush* in 1948 was a big deal! It was the first time so many Caribbean people had come to live in Britain in one go and was the start of lots more people arriving in the following years, all the way up until the 1970s. It's because of that first boat that the people who arrived in Britain over this time are known as the Windrush generation.

Even though people had travelled to Britain in response to adverts asking them to come, the new arrivals from the Caribbean often experienced racism. It was difficult to find decent accommodation or get jobs as some companies didn't want Black people working for them. There were children who got bullied at school, or treated as if they were less clever, all because of the colour of their skin.

It was these tensions that led to things like the Notting Hill riots, and other race riots and attacks, simply because people were not willing to be accepting of one another.

Today there are over 500,000 people living in the UK who arrived from Caribbean countries between 1948 and 1971. You might have heard people talk about the Windrush scandal recently? This is because some people who came to Britain as children were told – wrongly – that they were living in this country illegally! In 1971, they'd been told they could stay in this country permanently, but the government hadn't kept proper records. And as some people had never owned a UK passport (they might have come over on their parents' passports), they often didn't have all the documents the government required to prove they were UK residents.

In 2012, some people were told they needed official documents to prove they were entitled to things like NHS treatment, or disability and working benefits. But when people couldn't find their paperwork, or prove what they'd been asked to prove, they got packed off to immigration detention centres and faced deportation back to their country of origin! How unfair is that? Can you imagine what a shock that would be? For many people, Britain was the only country they'd known! It was their home, and where they'd built their lives.

There was a big outcry over how people were being treated and, in 2018, the government looked again at thousands of cases. This led to eighteen people of the Windrush generation receiving a formal apology for how they'd been treated. And rightly so! Compensation is still being sorted out, all these years later.

In the same year, the government announced that 22 June would be known as Windrush Day, a day to remember all the contributions of the Windrush generation and their descendants.

CLAUDIA JONES

COMMUNIST CO-CREATOR OF THE NOTTING HILL CARNIVAL

WHO WAS SHE? A journalist, activist and mother (co-creator) of the Notting Hill Carnival.

WHEN WAS SHE AROUND? 1915–1964

WHY IS SHE IMPORTANT? Claudia Jones launched Britain's first major Black newspaper and was a consistent driving force in campaigns for race equality in the UK. She also organized the first ever Notting Hill Carnival.

Claudia Jones was born Claudia Vera Cumberbatch in 1915 in Trinidad. Claudia's family had once been 'owned' by the Cumberbatch family, which is why they had taken their name (remember that descendants of slaves adopted their owners' names). When Claudia was born, Trinidad was still a British colony – and, as you'll know by now, that meant that the British controlled everything in that country. This included putting a colour bar in place that stopped Black people getting work and accessing many other opportunities.

One of the reasons Trinidad was really important to the British was because of the cocoa that was grown there. Cocoa meant chocolate, and when it was first produced, people just couldn't get enough of the sweet stuff! But two world wars and global money issues changed this and, at the time Claudia was growing up, cocoa wasn't selling as well as it had previously. Times were tough. So, Claudia's parents decided to leave their home and seek out better lives elsewhere.

Initially, they went alone – I guess to try and get things settled before their kids joined them. Aged eight, Claudia moved to New York to be with them, and that's when she took on the name

Jones. Although racism was pretty bad in the United States, the family hoped that things would be better than in Trinidad and they would at least find work. But growing up, Claudia's family didn't have much money at all and often lived in damp conditions, which wouldn't have been good for their health. After only five years of living in New York, Claudia's mum died from a really bad infection, aged just thirty-seven. A year later, Claudia herself ended up in hospital with tuberculosis – that's another horrible infection which can be made worse by bad living conditions.

Poor Claudia, losing her mum like that.

Claudia was really interested in politics from a young age. I read that Claudia reckoned the fact her mum had to work so hard as a machine worker in difficult conditions explained her early death. This may have some truth to it. So, knowing how hard her mum worked and realizing she was probably exploited, it's no surprise that Claudia wanted to try and make a difference. She could probably see all around her what was and wasn't fair for Black people – and injustices and inequality were not hard to find in the US at that time. Fair treatment didn't exist.

Claudia was clever and did well in school but ended up needing to work to earn money. She did a few jobs, working in laundry and retail, before joining a drama group. She got interested in journalism and wrote for a Harlem journal, which is where she became interested in activism. Her column was called 'Claudia's Comments'. She then joined the **COMMUNIST PARTY** and the Young Communist League.

QUICK FACTS: COMMUNISM

You might already know that different political parties have different systems and believe different things. Well, communism is the belief that no *one* person should own land or property, and instead the government should provide for us all and we should share everything equally. To some of you, that might sound good, but in the past, communist societies haven't really worked out.

Usually whoever is in power messes up, but maybe that's for another book!

Claudia started to become more politically aware and, through her journalism, she rose up the ranks until she was editing newsletters and attending rallies. She became a fantastic speaker, was passionate and articulate, and could hold an audience in the palm of her hand.

The Young Communist League changed its name to the American Youth for Democracy. Communism wasn't very popular in the US (and that's an understatement really!), so that was a clever bit of rebranding, if you ask me. Anyway, **Claudia became the editor for their monthly paper called *Spotlight* and, by 1938, she'd worked her way up to being editor of the left-wing paper the *Weekly Review*.**

At this point, Claudia had lived in the US for nearly fifteen years, but when she applied for US citizenship, she was refused. Communism was seen as a real threat in the US in those days and, through her political activities, Claudia was standing out. After all, she was announcing in her journalism that she thought the government was doing a bad job of running things. She wanted to put the power back in the hands of the working classes, and that wasn't a popular opinion with everyone.

Claudia toured the country and gave speeches. I can really get behind what she stood for – she was passionate about racial equality, getting fair treatment for the working classes, as well as for women, and she had to face all three circumstances. It's outrageous to think that all she really wanted was equal pay for equal work, and that was seen as revolutionary or dangerous! It was unusual for a Black woman who was skilled in public speaking and knew her politics to be so public at the time. When she spoke at gatherings, she'd stir people up, and she actually got arrested and sent to prison on Ellis Island for activities that were considered 'un-American' more than once! The stress of this might have contributed to the heart attack she had during one of her times in prison. She was only thirty-six at the time, which is pretty young to be having heart problems!

MOVING TO BRITAIN

Eventually, the US had enough of Claudia speaking out and, in 1955, she was forced to leave the country. She was supposed to go back to Trinidad because that was where she was from, but the government there refused to take her back in case she caused trouble.

For some people, being thrown out of one country, refused entry to another and then ending up somewhere totally unfamiliar might have slowed them down. But not Claudia! She got involved with politics and activism here, quickly realizing that the West Indian community in London struggled with racism too, and that she could make a difference and continue her fight for equality.

In 1958, using her knowledge of journalism, Claudia decided to start her own newspaper, the *West Indian Gazette and Afro-Asian Caribbean News*. This was the first weekly Black newspaper in the UK. She couldn't get funding for it (what a surprise!), so instead Claudia raised money by selling advertising space in the paper, and many people worked for free. The paper was an important part of her efforts organizing campaigns for equal rights in areas like employment, education and housing. Claudia believed she could raise awareness of what was happening, and that the community could change things by working together.

THE NOTTING HILL CARNIVAL

After the SS *Empire Windrush* brought many West Indians over in 1948, racism started growing in the UK. Throughout the 1950s, when more West Indians came here to work, areas became overcrowded. White men would complain about 'their' jobs being taken, or that they were being 'taken over'. The Black population was fed up with being discriminated against, especially by the police. During that time, the rent Black people had to pay was three or four times more that of white people, can you believe it!?

> How did they even get away with such unfair treatment?

So, with all of this going on, tensions were pretty high and there ended up being terrible fighting and riots in the streets across Britain. One of the most notorious of these riots happened in Notting Hill and, tragically, a young man called **Kelso Cochrane** was killed.

It was after this horrible event that Claudia and another woman had the idea to have a carnival to celebrate Caribbean culture and bring people together. They wanted to remind people of the good around them and to help them forget all the awful riots.

The first Caribbean Carnival took place in London in January 1959. It was held in St Pancras Town Hall and filmed by the BBC. There were many elements of carnival: calypso music, steel bands and costumes . . . all the things that we still see on the streets today during the Notting Hill Carnival.

It's because of that event that Claudia Jones is remembered as the mother of Notting Hill Carnival, but it's also thanks to another incredible woman called **Rhaune Laslett-O'Brien.** It was Rhaune who had the idea for a street festival in 1965/6. Some people have argued that because the Notting Hill Carnival is held on the streets, it's actually Rhaune's street festival which evolved into Notting Hill Carnival as we know it today, rather than Claudia's indoor event. However, I think it's enough for us to know and remember that the Carnival was founded by both these two extraordinary women, both of whom believed in equality.

Claudia died in her sleep on Christmas Eve 1964. She was only forty-nine, but she made a big impact even though she died so young.

She always stood up for what she believed in, and I really admire that. She often got into trouble, but always told the truth about how things were, so good on her!

TOP FIVE
FACTS ABOUT
CLAUDIA JONES

1. Claudia held Black beauty pageants to celebrate Black women at a time when many were made to think their beauty wasn't allowed to be celebrated. Many of the participants went on to have modelling and theatre careers.

2. Claudia is buried next to Karl Marx a very important guy in Communist history) in Highgate Cemetery.

3. The Notting Hill Carnival is now held every year and has had as many as two million visitors!

4. Claudia became executive secretary of the National Women's Commission in 1947.

5. In the USA there was a March on Washington for Jobs and Freedom in August 1963 (over 250,000 people attended!). Claudia was a leader for the one held in London a few days after Washington's one.

ASQUITH CAMILE XAVIER

TRAIN GUARD WHO FOUGHT DISCRIMINATION IN THE STATION

WHO WAS HE? The first non-white train guard at Euston railway station.

WHEN WAS HE AROUND? 1920–1980

WHY IS HE IMPORTANT? Asquith fought hard to do a job he loved and ended a colour bar that unfairly meant that men and women of colour could not work at some railway stations in Britain.

Asquith Camile Xavier was born on the island of Dominica in the West Indies on 18 July 1920. At this time, Dominica was a British colony and, when the British government asked for help to rebuild the country after the Second World War, Asquith was one of those who arrived as part of the Windrush generation.

The ship that Asquith came to Britain on docked on 16 April 1958 in Southampton. This was just ten years after the first passengers came over on the SS *Empire Windrush*.

He moved to Paddington in west London and got a job as a porter with British Rail (who ran the railways at the time), before moving up the ranks to become a guard at the Marylebone depot. When the freight link at Marylebone depot was closed in 1966, Asquith applied for a transfer to London Euston station. But there was a colour bar in place at Euston, which meant that they wouldn't give jobs to Black people. **This colour bar was unofficial, but was still very real, and Asquith had his application refused just because he was a Black man.**

Having an unofficial colour bar is something we'd now call institutionalized racism. This means that racism runs through all the different parts of the rules and regulations of companies or organizations, but that it might be quite hidden or unobvious. In this case, it meant that the railway management and unions had all informally agreed to make sure that non-white workers couldn't get any jobs that involved having contact with the public. So, racism was still defining who could and who couldn't be employed.

Obviously!

Asquith wasn't happy with this rule and, once again, like so many other Black men and women before him, he decided to campaign, trying to end the racial discrimination across British Rail.

A law called the Race Relations Act had been passed in 1965 which made it illegal to discriminate against people for

their colour, race, ethnicity or nationality in public places like cinemas or restaurants – but, somehow, the railways weren't thought of as public places. Asquith wasn't having that as an excuse for blatant discrimination! **So, with help from the National Union of Railwaymen (NUR) branch secretary, Jimmy Pendergast, and the Secretary of State for Transport, Barbara Castle, he made his case to British Rail.** In the end, Asquith's arguments were heard. In July, British Rail said they'd abandon the unofficial colour bar and on 15 August 1966, Asquith became the first non-white guard employed at Euston station.

This proves to me that individuals CAN make a difference, although it might not be easy.

Asquith shouldn't have had to fight for something so basic. The fact that he refused to accept what he'd been told meant that he overcame the discrimination he'd faced and got the job he wanted. And, even more importantly, he changed the law to ensure that other Black people also could get the jobs that they wanted!

With Asquith's job, the unofficial colour bar at Euston ended but, though that was an important change, there were still colour bars at other London railway stations, including Camden and Broad Street. With the law as it was, the government had limited options to stop those colour bars.

But change was being pushed for and **a new RACE RELATIONS ACT passed in 1968,** strengthened in part thanks to the help of Asquith's campaign at Euston. The new law stated it was now illegal to refuse people housing, employment or public services just because of their ethnic background. This was a big step forward because, as we know from some of the struggles of people we've talked about here, Black people had real problems finding work or accommodation while living here.

When Asquith started his new job at Euston, Ernest Drinnan was the station manager at the time, and he said: *'We expect Mr Xavier to fit in very well here . . . His record at Marylebone was exceptionally good and we know everyone here will take to him.'*

But sometimes the reality doesn't live up to the ideal and poor Asquith faced racial abuse from the public. He was sent hate mail, had threats made on his life and at one point, he needed police protection going to and from work.

Now, at last, Asquith's contribution to the fight for racial equality has been noticed and commemorated. He has two plaques – a small one that was put up at Euston station in 2016 and, on 24 September 2020, a beautiful black and gold plaque was unveiled in the waiting room of Chatham railway station, where Asquith caught the train to work every day.

FACT FILE: THE RACE RELATIONS ACTS

The Race Relations Act of December 1965 became the first UK law to address racial discrimination. It was supposed to outline clear laws that proved that everyone living in Britain had the legal right to be treated fairly.

In the late 1960s, nearly one million immigrants lived here and often they were treated shockingly. It's quite hard for us to understand now because discrimination is illegal and we know it's wrong, but at that time, many people were refused jobs and places to live. They were made to wait longer in queues to be served, or refused to be served at all just because of the colour of their skin. If you had a 'foreign'-sounding name, you could get your job or housing application rejected! There was nothing you could do and no way to fight back. I can't believe how recent all this was!

But this 1965 law made it a criminal offence to discriminate against somebody because of the colour of their skin, race, ethnicity or nationality.

As we all know by now, just because something is made law doesn't mean that everyone is going to listen.

There was still clear racism and discrimination in British society. Because it became obvious that many incidents of racism were still happening, in 1968 a *new* Race Relations Act was created. And this one made it illegal for people to be refused housing or a job because of their background.

And, in 1976, a *third* Race Relations Act went even further in trying to make things fair for minorities. Also, the Commission for Racial Equality was established. Both the 1968 and 1976 acts addressed how discrimination was dealt with, but – and I hate to say it, but it's true – as we can see from the way Black football players were harassed after England lost the European Championship final in 2021, racism still exists in this country. There is much more that needs be done.

Years after the landmark case of Stephen Lawrence (a young Black teenager who was murdered in 1993), there was an inquiry into how his murder was handled by the police, and racist attitudes and beliefs were found within the Metropolitan Police itself. It's shocking that an organization dedicated to helping protect people and solve crimes was biased in how they treated Black people. This was so unfair that it led to the 1976 law being changed – the Race Relations (Amendment) Act in 2000 included, for the first time, the police. This amended act enhanced and broadened the 1976 act.

Of course, it's not just race that can be a reason for why people are discriminated against. So, in 2010, the Equality Act was created, which covered gender, disability, religion, sexual orientation and age too (among other things!). This law explains very clearly how not to treat someone and exactly what is against the law.

With the murder of George Floyd, the Black Lives Matter movement and the COVID-19 pandemic, people's awareness of racism is growing. More people who experience discrimination feel able to come forward to share their experiences, and thankfully now there are many organizations and charities who work hard to get rid of racial discrimination and support those experiencing it.

AMAZING HERE AND NOW

SNAPSHOTS OF PEOPLE YOU NEED TO KNOW ABOUT!

At the start of our whirlwind journey through the past, I told you that history isn't something that stands still. Which is why throughout this book I've shared interviews with people you might have heard of who are making history themselves.

But there are SO many more Black people doing incredible things right now who we don't always hear about. And if going *Black in Time* has taught me anything, we all need to make sure that we're shouting from the rooftops about people's lives and achievements. So, now we're right up to date, I'm going to take one last moment to tell you about some more amazing-here-and-now stars. They may not all be in the history books (yet!) but tell others about what they've achieved and use their actions to inspire you!

JACQUELINE MCKENZIE, *a human-rights lawyer has won recognition for her work seeking justice for victims of the Windrush scandal.*

Jacqueline has family in the Caribbean and was educated in Grenada. Her legal work focuses on immigration and citizenship cases, and she started her career working at Hackney Council in London in 1987.

Even before the Windrush scandal came to everyone's attention in 2018, Jacqueline had already been helping clients born in the Caribbean with their citizenship claims, so she had her eye on the ball. For over twenty-seven years, Jacqueline has worked in the area of civil liberties, crime and immigration.

Jacqueline worked on many Windrush cases – over two hundred – and founded the Organization of Migration Advice and Research. She also works as a diversity consultant and is a member of the Independent Advisory Group for the Windrush Lessons Learned Review, which was established to examine and analyze evidence and progress of the Review.

WINSOME PINNOCK *is an award-winning playwright and academic. Her work has been produced internationally and on the British stage since 1985.*

Winsome Pinnock was born in 1961 in north London. Her parents were from Smithville, Jamaica. She studied drama and English at Goldsmiths, University of London, and wrote 'in secret', she says, while studying. She says she struggled to get supported because of the colour of her skin and that Black playwrights weren't treated the same as their white counterparts.

She went on to study for a master's degree in modern literature at Birkbeck, University of London, and then went into academia because it was a more secure profession than writing. She managed to balance both careers and has had over fifteen plays produced.

Winsome remembers being the only Black person on her course at university. Of course, things have changed now, although still not as much as we might like.

Winsome was the first Black British female writer to have a play produced by the National Theatre, which is pretty amazing! What's not so amazing is that it was only in 1988, which probably sounds *ages* ago to you, but think about how long ago some of the people we've been talking about lived, and how slow that shows progress has been!

The *Guardian* newspaper interviewed Winsome in 2018 and she said:

'I never imagined I'd ever have a play on. I grew up in Islington, in the poor bit, in a single-parent household and I was educated in the inner city. When I was told I was the first Black woman to have a play on at the National Theatre, I thought, "That's great, that's progress." But then I thought, "Why did it take so long?"'

Exactly my thoughts, Winsome!

SISLIN FAY ALLEN, *Britain's first Black policewoman.*

Sislin Fay Allen was born in Jamaica and came to Britain in 1961. She was only twenty-nine when she joined the London Metropolitan Police in 1968 and became the first Black female police officer. Talking about slow progress – I bet you can't guess when the first Black *male* police officer in Britain was, can you? Well, I'll tell you – he was called John Kent and he was a policeman in the 1830s! Yup, what a surprise, yet again being a woman *and* Black meant even slower progress – you had sexism to fight against as well as racism!

Sislin was working at Croydon's Queen's Hospital as a nurse, but after seeing an advert for police officers, she decided to make a career change.

'I was on my lunch break and during that time I was going through the paper. I saw this advert and they were recruiting police officers,' she said in a Sky News interview in October 2020. 'So, I looked at it and thought, "why not?". I cut the advert out and put it in my pocket and said, "when I have time,

I'll fill it out.". After I finished work around seven, I went home, filled it out and posted it off. I thought nothing of it . . . I didn't set out to make history!'

After stating on the initial application form that she was Black, a few weeks later, Sislin was invited to the next stage: an interview.

'On the selection day there were so many people there, the hall was filled with the young men. There were ten women and I was the only Black person.'

She had to pass a strict medical to make sure she was fit and healthy enough, as well as taking exams. After she passed, she started work at Fell Road police station in Croydon.

'The first day on the beat in Croydon was daunting, but it wasn't too bad because I went out with an officer . . . People were curious to see a Black woman there in uniform walking up and down, but I had no problem at all, not even from the public . . . I remember on the day I joined; I nearly broke a leg trying to run away from reporters. I soon realized then that I was a history maker, but I didn't set out to make history; I just wanted a change of direction.'

After a year in Croydon, Sislin went to Scotland Yard, the headquarters of the London police force, before transferring to Norbury police station. Luckily, she didn't see the hate mail, as the unpleasant letters were kept from her by the Met. This was probably a good thing, as if she'd read them, she might have considered quitting her job.

In 1972, Sislin left Britain and went to live in Jamaica with her husband and two children. But she didn't give up doing what she loved and joined the Jamaican police force.

In October 2020, Sislin was given a special lifetime achievement award for her accomplishments by the National Black Police Association, celebrating Black, Asian and minority ethnic officers.

Dame Cressida Dick, former Commissioner of the Metropolitan Police (aka the big boss of the London police) described Sislin as 'a pioneer of her time and an inspiration for many'. Sislin died on 5 July 2021 aged eighty-three at her home in St Ann, Jamaica.

Sislin was someone who truly forged a path for Black women who came after her. So much so that, in 2019, the Metropolitan Police used her image on posters to encourage more Black women to join.

Figures from that year showed that only three per cent of Metropolitan Police officers were from Black and ethnic minority backgrounds – a tiny amount!

If we don't see Black police officers on the street, or Black firemen and women, or Black judges, lawyers and doctors, then thoughts can unconsciously creep in that perhaps certain careers are off limits for Black people. But that isn't true! Black children can grow up to be whatever they want to be, and that's why I think it's important to include people from here and now who've made a difference by being bold in their achievements.

OLIVETTE OTELE,
*the UK's first Black
female history
professor.*

Now, it seems like a
really good idea to end
this book by talking to
an historian, and a Black
woman nonetheless!

Olivette Otele was born in 1970 in Cameroon,
and then grew up in Paris. She remembers first
getting passionate about history by listening to
her grandma in Cameroon telling her stories about
when the country was ruled by the British, the
French and the Germans. Olivette did a degree in
literature and history at Paris-Sorbonne University
in 1998.

Olivette gave an interview to the *TES* magazine in
2018, when she talked a bit about her background:

'I was influenced by a strong, kind and independent
grandmother who lived on the edge of the
rainforest. She taught me to love myself (not to be
in love with myself), to share love with others, to
protect the environment and to respect all living
creatures.'

She sounds like a great grandmother to have!

In 1999, Olivette left Paris with her family to live in Wales, but she continued to travel regularly to France for her PhD and then to take up a role as an Associate Professor in Paris. Then, in 2018 she moved fully to the UK to become a professor of history at Bath Spa University. Becoming a professor is the highest academic position you can get in this country, so she really is a Black woman at the top of her game!

In May 2019, Olivette was made Vice-President of the Royal Historical Society and in 2020, was appointed Professor of the History of Slavery at the University of Bristol. Bristol was a leading slave port in the eighteenth century. She has researched the effects of colonial and post-colonial pasts for over twenty years. She looks at how memory, history and politics all connect.

When asked what advice would she give to her younger self, Olivette replied: *'No advice. Just words of encouragement:*

"You are right to believe in the goodness of people. Keep doing what you do; working hard, loving, laughing, forgiving and doing your bit might not change the whole world, but it will change you for the best.'"

Hopefully her work will help make history a more inclusive subject for all, which is exactly what I hope this book will do in its own small way, too!

Olivette helped me by reading this book to check Emma and I had all of our facts straight, and I also got the chance to ask her some burning questions! So, let's hear from Olivette herself . . .

AMAZING HERE AND NOW
OLIVETTE OTELE

What inspired you to become a historian? If you hadn't, what would you be?

Growing up, I was amazed by my grandmother's ability to tell stories in a way that captivated all of us and always left us wanting to know more. I knew from a very young age that I wanted to express myself in a way that resonated with people. I wanted to be a dancer, and later on a novelist, then I wanted to work on poetry. After a joint degree in literature and history, I decided to do a Master's in history, then wanted to do a doctorate on Welsh poets. However, a controversy about the role of the city of Bristol in transatlantic enslavement shifted my perception of the past. I wanted to know why humanity finds the past so painful that we try to hide parts of it. I wanted to know why the stories of people of African descent were always about pain and destruction, when the stories that my grandmother used to share with me, of living in

Cameroon, were much more joyful. So, I decided to tell the stories of the past in a way that was accessible to lots of people. They are stories of pain but also collaborations, endurance and liberation.

How did you feel when you became the first Black female history professor?

It was both pure joy and pain. I worked really hard for years and I did think that I deserved the title. I only wished I was not the only one in Britain, especially in 2018. It should have happened before. There are many deserving Black women around me and being the first one to become a professor in history, and remaining the only one for a few years, felt very lonely. We need more Black female professors and there are so many women who should be promoted.

I've written about lots of amazing Black people in this book. If you could go back in time and meet a historical figure, who would it be? Or would you love to travel to a particular time period?

History has not been kind to Black women. Now is probably the time I prefer to live in. However, if I really had to go back in time, I'd like to meet a fantastic educator who gained her PhD when she was well into her sixties, an African-American woman called Anna Julia Cooper. I would have also loved to meet Queen Nzinga of Ndongo and Matamba, who lived in the 16th and 17th centuries in present-day Angola, a country on the west coast of Africa. She was a military leader, a diplomat and a powerful woman, who fought against Portuguese invasion for as long as she could, making alliances when necessary but always defending her people. She could be found on the battlefield even in her sixties!

We've also seen in this book how opinions and thoughts on race have changed over time (or, in some cases, not!). Do you think your view of the present is shaped by what you know from your studies? How important do you think learning about history is to understanding today?

My present-day views are definitely shaped by my studies. I learned a lot and history has taught me humility. We are standing on the shoulders of great women and men who made our present more bearable in many ways. Learning about history, and especially global history, shows us that the history of humanity started long before the periods we tend to focus on. The history of ancient Africa, or what is known as pre-colonial Africa, is just as important as the history of ancient China or classical Greece. Populations interacted long before Africa and Europe were known as different continents.

We have to learn from the past to understand many things today, but many stories of the past have not been completely or accurately recorded, so it is also important to bring to the surface histories that have been forgotten so that we can have a fuller picture of our common past.

What would your best piece of advice be for any readers who want to become historians?

I would tell them to read about all kinds of histories as much as they can, because history is about making connections with all kinds of communities, as much as it is about understanding the local, national and global contexts and how they influence events and shape the way people tell the stories or remember the past. They have to be willing to read and learn about their own history as much as other people's. They have to be willing to let curiosity guide them. It's as fascinating to learn about animal history as it is to read how objects, from coins to paintings, monuments to spices, influence the way we see the world and other people's cultures.

From a historian's perspective, do you think I'll go down in history?!

You definitely will. You are one of the very few Black women we see on British national television. Your presence tells children and young people from minority ethnic backgrounds in Britain that they deserve to be seen and appreciated, too. That shows them that they can achieve many things, and just like you, they also have a lot to share. As far as grown-ups like me are concerned, it is such a joy to see and hear you speak, because of the humanity and warmth you bring to your audience. It's magical!

THE FINAL WORD FROM ME

Where did all this come from, you might ask? Why did I want to create this book? Why do I think it's so important for all of us to know the stories of these people?

Well, really, I started off by remembering a play I saw with my mum and brother when I was about fourteen. It was called **Black Heroes in the Hall of Fame** and was exactly what it sounds like – a play all about Black people who had been trailblazers and heroes. I remember just being totally blown away by hearing about these people that I'd never known about before – like **Garrett Morgan**, the man who'd invented the traffic light. That play was the first time I'd ever seen such incredible Black people mentioned on stage. I was so inspired, and so were my mum and brother – so much so that we all went back to see the play again the very next day!

> That moment was a total eye-opener for me about how biased history and the things we're told can be. Someone has made a choice about who to include in history books, whose lives are the most important, who we should know about and who gets left out entirely.

I'd absolutely love this book to have the same sort of impact on you that the play had on me and for it to be part of the conversation that ensures things start changing – that we look again at history and don't exclude people just because of the colour of their skin, or for any other reason.

So when I was thinking about my final thoughts on this project and how to express everything that I've learned while working with my writing partner Emma on the book, I couldn't quite believe how amazing it's been.

I've learned that we can achieve whatever we put our minds to. When we see role models who look like us achieving great things, then we believe that we can too. **Phillis Wheatly**, the poet, aimed high. She wanted to write poetry, believed in her dreams, and achieved exactly what she wanted.

And look at me, I never believed I could get on to prime-time telly – but that's exactly what I'm doing now!

And I've loved **Mary Seacole** ever since my mum told me about her, because she said I have a caring nature just like her. **George Bridgetower** inspired me to persuade my son Aidan to start playing the violin, then he also went on to the cello!

Now of course he's into F1 race-car driving . . . but at least Lewis Hamilton is still an inspiration!

I want to pass all this encouragement down to the generations ahead of me. What's great is that you'll all have more knowledge and awareness of Black people in the UK and what a difference they've made. This book (and others like it) highlights and brings Black history out into the open. And there's no need to be embarrassed if you don't know these names. I'm forty-six, and I'm still learning about Black history. I believe that we're always learning. You can pass this book along to your friends, parents, siblings, aunts, uncles or other family members too – why not read it together? Hopefully you'll agree that I've helped shine a light on these people, and we can't allow that light to be dulled by history books again. This book is here as a gift for everyone to learn about these amazing people. We don't want them to be hidden any more! We can put these Black people from history on our school curriculum. We can include them in history lessons at school, so that every child understands and appreciates that not only have Black people always been here, but that they were just as important, talented, intelligent, special and AWESOME as anyone else. All the people in the book paved the way for many more successful Black people.

It's not a perfect world yet, but these trailblazers have shown us what can be done.

And the people in this book are just the start! There are SO many more incredible Black people from our history that we don't know about but should. So, don't stop here, get out there and get discovering!

And listen – all you future writers and historians reading this – don't forget to keep our legacy alive!

love, Alison xx

GET READING!

Ha! You thought I'd gone, didn't you? Well, not quite yet – I'm just popping back to give you a list of some reading you might want to check out to learn more about the people in this book, hear about some people that I've not had time to talk about, or inspire you to start making history yourself. Black history is wide and varied, which means there's loads more to discover than one book can hold. Here's some suggestions of where you might want to start.

BLACK HISTORY

The Black History Book: Big Ideas Simply Explained (DK)

Timelines from Black History: Leaders, Legends, Legacies (DK)

Black and British: A Short, Essential History (David Olusoga, Macmillan Children's Books)

Black History Matters (Robin Walker, Franklin Watts)

BLACK FIGURES

99 Immigrants Who Made Britain Great (Louis Stewart and Naomi Kenyon, Canbury Press)

The *Extraordinary Lives* series (various authors, Puffin)

Little Leaders: Bold Women in Black History

Little Leaders: Exceptional Black Men in History (Vashti Harrison, Puffin)

Little People, BIG DREAMS series (Maria Isabel Sanchez Vegara and various illustrators, Frances Lincoln Children's Books)

100 Great Black Britons (Patrick Vernon, Robinson)

The History of Mary Prince: A West Indian Slave (autobiography, Penguin Classics)

ACTIVISM AND ACTION

Silence is Not An Option (Stewart Lawrence, Scholastic)

Young, Gifted and Black: Meet 52 Black Heroes from Past and Present (Jamia Wilson and illustrated by Andrea Pippins, Wide Eyed Editions)

You Are a Champion (Marcus Rashford, Macmillan Children's Books)

Black, Listed: Black British Culture Explored (Jeffrey Boakye, Dialogue Books)

FICTION

Windrush Child (Benjamin Zephaniah, Scholastic)

VOICES series (including a story about Ted Fanque written by Emma, who helped write this book!) (various authors, Scholastic)

Coming to England (Floella Benjamin, Macmillan Children's Books)

Bedtime Stories: Beautiful Black Tales from the Past (various authors, Scholastic)

Hey You! An empowering celebration of growing up Black (Dapo Adelo and various illustrators, Puffin)

Happy Here: 10 stories from Black British authors & illustrators (various authors and illustrators, Knights Of Media)

WEBSITES

100 Great Black Britons
www.100greatblackbritons.com/list.html

The Black Presence in Britain – Black British History
www.blackpresence.co.uk

Black Londoners Through Time
www.museumoflondon.org.uk/families/black-londoners-through-time

BlackPast
www.blackpast.org

A Mighty Girl – 99 Books about Extraordinary Mighty Black Girls and Women
www.amightygirl.com/blog?p=14276

Black Plaque Project – Telling the Untold Sides of History
www.blackplaqueproject.com

The Black Heroes of Science
www.blackhistorymonth.org.uk/article/section/science-and-medicine/black-heroes-science

ACKNOWLEDGEMENTS

This book has been a real passion project for me. I've always wanted to produce something that I would have loved to have had as a child, and now my wish is to give it to children everywhere.

This is also for all children who want to learn more about their British history. Please enjoy and pass the knowledge on to your friends and family.

Special thanks to Emma Norry, who really has worked so hard on this book – I honestly owe her everything. Emma, I know this book has been such an investment for you and I really appreciate the amount of work you have dedicated to it. Thanks for being my partner and helping me so much with the facts and research.

Thanks to everyone at Puffin for all your guidance and support, especially to my editor Jane Griffiths for making it such a dream, Sarah Connelly for getting the words in the right places and to Alice Todd and Dan Newman for making those words look so brilliant. And a really big thanks to the very talented Tinuke Fagborun for her incredible illustrations, both throughout the book and on the cover – I love them!

Thanks to my inspirations Becca Barr, Jack Hunter Blair, Dru, Lily and Vicky. Mariam Hussain, Ryan

Samuda, Anna Manton, Sue Walton, Noleen Golding, Satmohan Panesar, and everyone who worked on the documentary *Alison Hammond: Back to School* for ITV, which sparked my interest in sharing Black history.

Big thanks to all the historical figures, both those featured and not featured in this book – without your legacy this certainly wouldn't be possible. Thank you also to all the amazing Here and Now contributors who answered my probing questions! It's been great hearing your thoughts about the past, and I'm excited about the future for Black kids, knowing that there are incredible role models like all of you to look up to. Special thanks to Olivette Otele, who not only answered my questions but read through the whole of this book to make sure that Emma and I had our facts totally straight!

Thanks to all the teachers who may use this book. You are the link to preserving this part of history and allowing it to live on and not be hidden in the shadows. I am extremely grateful to you.

Lastly, I would like to thank my mum for taking me to see *Black Heroes in the Hall of Fame* at the Alexandra Theatre in Birmingham all those years ago. Thanks for setting my fire alight with regards to Black history and knowing the truth. You will always be in my heart, Mum. xx

ABOUT THE AUTHORS

ALISON HAMMOND has been a much-loved fixture on British television for two decades. She joined *This Morning* in 2002 and has since secured some of the most watched – and loved – celebrity interviews ever. She's tap-danced with Renée Zellweger, rapped with Will Smith, jammed with Russell Crowe and been serenaded by Hugh Jackman.

In 2021, she became one of *This Morning*'s main hosts, alongside Dermot O'Leary, and appeared on a new BBC Saturday-night primetime entertainment show, *I Can See Your Voice*, alongside fellow judges Amanda Holden and Jimmy Carr, and host Paddy McGuinness.

From her rise to fame on Channel 4's *Big Brother* in 2002 to her appearances on *I'm a Celebrity . . . Get Me Out of Here!*, *Strictly Come Dancing* and *Celebrity Great British Bake Off*, Alison's warmth, honesty and joy have made her one of the most popular presenters on TV today.

Follow Alison Hammond on Twitter: @AlisonHammond and Instagram: alisonhammond55

EMMA NORRY is an author who writes fiction and non-fiction for children. She is passionate about equal representation and diversity. Her first book, *Son of the Circus* (Scholastic, 2019), is part of a series that shows readers that Black and brown people have always been a part of British history. *Son of the Circus*, set in Victorian times, blended fact and fiction by using Pablo Fanque (the first Black circus owner) and his son Ted as inspiration. Emma has also written *Amber Undercover* (OUP, 2021) - a fun action-adventure spy story for ages 10+. She has many short stories in anthologies: *Happy Here* (Knights Of Media, 2021), *The Place for Me: Stories from the Windrush* (Scholastic, 2020) and *The Very Merry Murder Club* (Farshore, 2021). Emma's non-fiction includes biographies of Lionel Messi (Scholastic, 2020) and Nelson Mandela (Puffin, 2020). A two-book middle-grade fantasy series launches in 2023. Emma can be found on Twitter at @elnorry_writer or her website elnorry.com